JANET MELROSE &
SHERYL NORMANDEAU

The Prairie Gardener's Go-To for

Herbs

TOUCHWOOD

TouchWood Editions
touchwoodeditions.com

The information in this book is true and complete to the best of the authors' knowledge. All recommendations are made without guarantee on the part of the authors or the publisher.

Copy edited by Paula Marchese

Proofread by Meg Yamamoto

Designed by Tree Abraham

Photos by Janet Melrose and Sheryl Normandeau, with the following exceptions: p. 27 (MSPhotographic / shutterstock.com), p. 45 (Mongkol Phisutsrisakul / shutterstock. com), p. 59 (Linda Hall / shutterstock.com), p. 61 (Alexas_Fotos / pixabay.com), p. 69 (gefrorene_wand / pixabay.com), p. 75 (Hans / pixabay.com), p. 87 (courtesy of Curtis Reynolds), p. 131 (Sharky Photography / shutterstock.com).

CATALOGUING DATA AVAILABLE FROM LIBRARY AND ARCHIVES CANADA

ISBN 9781771514286 (print)

ISBN 9781771514293 (electronic)

TouchWood Editions acknowledges that the land on which we live and work is within the traditional territories of the Lkwungen (Esquimalt and Songhees), Malahat, Pacheedaht, Scia'new, T'sou-ke, and W̱SÁNEĆ (Pauquachin, Tsartlip, Tsawout, and Tseycum) peoples.

We acknowledge the financial support of the Government of Canada through the Canada Book Fund, and the province of British Columbia through the Book Publishing Tax Credit.

This book was produced using FSC®-certified, acid-free papers, processed chlorine free, and printed with soya-based inks.

Printed in China

28 27 26 25 24   1 2 3 4 5

Dedicated to all prairie gardeners

Introduction 7

Introduction

What is an herb? It seems like such a straightforward question. We all know what an herb is, don't we? But as soon as we start to reply, we pause. It's not as easy as those flakes of parsley or thyme that flavour our food so enticingly. We often use herbs for culinary purposes, but what about all the herbs used by herbalists for medicinal purposes? Or the ones we use to calm or invigorate ourselves? Or the ones that connect us to our spiritual side? There are even herbs that can be harmful to life if used for that purpose.

Going beyond the uses we have for herbs, we need to consider what sort of plants are herbs. Are they just annual ones that go from seed to seed in one season? Or are there also herbaceous perennial ones? What about trees and shrubs?

By the time we have thought about all the answers to those questions, we are in a right muddle. But it doesn't need to be that way if we go right back to the roots of the matter: language, that is, not botanically speaking. Our English word "herb" is derived from the Latin *herba*, simply meaning grass or green crops.[1]

The Oxford Dictionary gives us two meanings of the word "herb" that together are most useful and provide boundaries for the scope of this book. As a noun, an herb is any plant with leaves, seeds, or flowers used for flavouring, food, medicine, or perfume.[2] It is also any seed-bearing plant that does not have a woody stem and dies down to the ground after flowering.[3] For the purposes of this book, we will generally stick with this definition, occasionally straying to encompass a few roots considered herbs in common use, and cover a few trees and shrubs that we use as herbals.

Herbs are not just used for culinary purposes, though certainly their role in making our cuisine both delightfully delicious to eat and culturally diverse cannot be overstated. Many are also high in nutrients, minerals, vitamins, and antioxidants necessary to maintain health.

We tend to forget in our modern world that medicine as we know it began with ancient peoples gathering and experimenting with various plants as remedies to alleviate pain and other symptoms of illness and injury. Apothecaries were stocked with plants grown in botanical gardens. Herbalists were wise women and men, revered by their neighbours for their knowledge of plants and their abilities to preserve health as well as restore it. Today, herbalism is enjoying a renaissance around the world.

Herbs have been used for spiritual purposes since time immemorial. They form parts of rituals and ceremonies for people and cultures everywhere. Herbs, as well as spices, are the backbone of aromatherapy. Their sweet fragrances and pungent odours are used to relieve stress, energize, cleanse the spirit, and enhance one's moods. Simply running one's fingers through lavender or sniffing sage is enough to validate the effectiveness of herbs as aromatherapy.

Herbs have other roles, too. They are used in cosmetics as well as for dyeing, not to mention their ornamental value in our gardens. They are used in companion planting as well as in Integrated Pest Management.

Not only do herbs have multiple and overlapping roles, but they also convey singular benefits for the gardener and cook in us all. Growing our own herbs saves us money, we get to enjoy their superior taste and other properties, and we broaden our minds and knowledge. In the landscape, herbs can have multiple functions. They bring biodiversity to our gardens as well as provide layers for a

resilient garden, from ground covers to semi-shrubs, hedges, focal points, and more. They can even replace a lawn or at least a section of it, if you so choose. Many herbs suffer little to no damage from maundering insects, birds, and mammals, coming as they do with their own defences against the animal world. Even more importantly, most herbs are able to adapt to our ever warmer and drier climate on the prairies.

Lastly, and this is important, they are a delight to grow and care for. The world of herbs awaits![4] —SHERYL NORMANDEAU & JANET MELROSE

8

What is the difference between an herb and a spice?

If we start with a definition of an herb being an aromatic plant where we use the green parts (leaves, and sometimes flowers), either fresh or dried, then a spice is all the other parts of the plant—roots, stems, bark, berries, seeds, and seed receptacles. I often think of herbs and spices on the colour spectrum where the herbs are the cool greens, and the spices are the yellows, browns, reds, and oranges. That seems simple.

So cinnamon is a spice, being the bark of its tree. Garlic, ditto, as we use the bulb. Dill (*Anethum graveolens*) and cilantro (*Coriandrum sativum*) are herbs because we use the leaves and immature flowers. Mint (*Mentha* spp.)—ditto.

But wait a minute! We also use the fresh leaves and scapes of garlic to flavour our foods. And we use dill and cilantro seeds too, and cilantro is also known as the spice coriander when we gather the mature seeds. So, is garlic (*Allium sativum*) an herb or a spice or a vegetable? What about dill, cilantro/coriander, and fennel (*Foeniculum vulgare*)?

Shall I throw in another wrinkle? Pepper (*Piper nigrum*) is a spice as it is the dried berries we grind. But pepper is also a fruit when it is a species in the *Capsicum* genus, even though we often think of them as vegetables. We don't think of bell peppers as a spice, nor even the hotter ones like the habanero. But what about paprika, made from dried *Capsicum annuum* fruit pods? That is a spice for sure, isn't it?

We do love the circles we can go around and around when we try to fit plants into our artificial categories. As Kermit says, it's not easy being green—if you are a frog or an herb, that is!—JM

Designing with Herbs

1

What is a pot herb? How is it different from a salad herb?

We sure do love putting our plants into neat pigeonholes for some rather arbitrary reasons, but in these instances, they also convey a sense of their main purpose or use. So, then, a pot herb is any herb used specifically for culinary reasons, mostly to season or flavour our food. The herbs that immediately come to mind, such as our mint, rosemary, dill, and so forth, fall into this category. But a pot herb can also be those plants that aren't considered as such. Pot marigold (*Calendula officinalis*) can be the star of this category as we can use the petals to colour and flavour our food. It is occasionally referred to as "poor man's saffron" for the lovely yellowy colour it imparts to rice. Other pot herbs are starflower or borage (*Borago officinalis*) as well as nasturtium (*Tropaeolum majus*). These are all edible flowers, but their foliage may also be consumed, either raw or cooked.

In fact, another definition for pot herbs is those herbs that we cook as greens. Into this pot go stinging nettle (*Urtica dioica*), horseradish (*Armoracia rusticana*), dandelion (*Taraxacum officinale*), and dock (*Rumex obtusifolius*) as well as its cousin common sorrel (*R. acetosa*). A number of so-called weeds, such as purslane (*Portulaca oleracea*), common mallow (*Malva neglecta*), and, of course, dandelion, are also pot herbs.

Which leads us to the other pigeonhole, that of salad herbs. Well, these are mostly those herbs where we would include the leaves in a salad as a nice touch, but not a main ingredient. Often that is because their taste is strong, many times bitter. But also, if we eat too much of them at a time, they can impair our digestive systems due to the chemicals they contain. Spinach contains oxalic acid in mild quantities, but dock has much higher levels and we all know about rhubarb (*Rheum rhabarbarum*) leaves. I love including fresh dandelion leaves in salads as they are similar to endive. I also use nasturtium, borage, and pot marigold leaves in small amounts. Sorrel is perhaps the poster child for a salad herb. With a lovely lemony taste that is often the first edible to be harvested in spring, it is great in those early spring green salads. Children love it too; at a school I work with, students are addicted to it as they eagerly await the first leaves of "lemon leaf" as they call it. If a whole lot of kids munch on it happily, then we too can experiment with all these pot and salad herbs![1] —JM

Stinging nettle must be cooked before you can consume it.

I want to grow herbs in containers. What type of growing medium should I use?

Use whatever is easiest for you to manage and is within your budget. You can purchase a commercial brand of potting or container mix (not a seed-starting mix). Don't bother with any of the add-ons that are on the market: you don't need water-retaining crystals, and there is no need to spend extra money on additions of mycorrhizal fungi. Don't buy a mix that is overloaded with peat moss or coir fibre as it will dry out way too quickly and has no nutritional value whatsoever. You'll want your mix to contain a good portion of organic matter in the form of compost, and it should contain topsoil.

Avoid using garden soil in your containers. It's dense, heavy, and easily compacts into a cement-like consistency that isn't friendly to plant roots.

You can also make your own soil mix for containers. One common recipe is:
1 part compost
1 part topsoil
1 part perlite or pumice
1 part coir fibre or peat moss

This recipe can be modified as you see fit. (I know that for environmental reasons some gardeners are gravitating toward less peat use.) You can mix in a handful or two of other ingredients as well, including alfalfa meal, feather meal, fish meal, greensand, and vermicompost. These will add nutrients and help with the structure of your growing mediums, increasing porosity and water-holding capacity. —SN

Can I mix different types of herbs in one container?

Certainly, you can! The sight of a beautiful container with a mix of leaf forms, colours, and sizes along with a heady aroma will gladden a weary heart. However, the temptation is to plant up some of your favourite herbs in one pot because those are the ones that either you use the most or are part of a recipe, or even because those were the ones that were available when you put together your pot. I have been guilty of all three reasons and I always slap my forehead come mid-summer when a couple of plants in the container are doing great, another is okay, and two have pooped out and gone to plant heaven.

The difficulty of mixing herbs, usually culinary, in the same container is that we need to consider each plant's requirements for sunlight exposure, both intensity and duration. Lavender (*Lavandula* spp.) loves full sun but cilantro not so much, nor bay laurel (*Laurus nobilis*), whose foliage experiences sun scald easily. We also need to think of each plant's requirements for water, with some being native to arid soil conditions and others requiring a moisture-retentive growing medium, whereas still others want their feet in an almost soggy medium. Rosemary (*Salvia rosmarinus*) loves drier soils but try putting watercress (*Nasturtium officinale*) in the same container. Both will struggle.

Consider the type of soil each herb prefers. Some do best in soils that are on the acidic side of life (<6 pH) whereas others want alkaline conditions (>7 pH). The usual growing medium for containers is peat moss or coir fibre with compost and other amendments. This mix is slightly acidic depending on the type of peat used or if coir is the base. For instance, bay laurel prefers alkaline soil but garlic chives (*Allium tuberosum*) want acidic soils. Different herbs also like different soil types, from almost gritty sand that drains water freely to spongy, peaty mixes that retain moisture. Lemon balm (*Melissa officinalis*) wants that sandy, gritty mix but mint doesn't. Most herbs are fairly forgiving, but it is a wise gardener that learns who likes what best.

We also need to factor in our herbs' hardiness in our climate. Many are very tender and will suffer damage even in summer should we have a cold spell, whereas others are tough as nails. Why pull everyone inside for an unseasonable frost, when the hardy types are thrilled it's cooler? I am thinking basil (*Ocimum basilicum*) or pineapple sage (*Salvia elegans*) as just a couple of examples that hate a chill, but sorrel laps it up.

Also a consideration is which herbs behave themselves in a container and which do not. Some will literally take over the entire container, both roots and upper structures. Others are tidy and stay where they are put, with nice compact growth. The infamous one, of course, is mint. Put it in a container and the others will automatically leave town.

Herbs that really need to be in ground shouldn't be planted in containers. Any that have taproots or fleshy roots grow best in the garden bed, as well as those that will want to develop large root systems. They won't be happy in the constrained surroundings of a container, nor will their companions.

An attractive container also needs to be in proportion, with each herb an appropriate size relative to the others. Ensure that the container, too, is of the size and proportion to both ensure that the herbs within have optimum growing conditions and present those beautiful plants at their best. Thankfully, there are many species and cultivars to choose from.[2]—**JM**

Mint is both delicious and rampaging. Grow it in a container to spare yourself the headache of having to dig it out of spaces where it is unwanted for years to come.

Can I grow herbs in raised beds?

Absolutely! There are a few things to consider before you get started, however. The depth of soil in your bed is important for some herbs. Perennial lovage (*Levisticum officinale*), for example, has seriously deep roots that need plenty of space. It may be better to put it into an in-ground bed if your raised bed is shallow.

Some herbs spread aggressively. Mint is a classic example. If you plant mint in a raised bed, be prepared for it to take over the entire bed (or perhaps that is your intention?). It is perennial on the prairies, and you will be digging it out for an eternity (unless you're in it for the mint juleps). There is little chance that you'll be able to plant anything alongside it that can compete favourably.

Garlic is often planted in raised beds (due to the fact that I don't have a garden with in-ground beds, it's the only place I grow it!), but in climates such as mine in Calgary, where we have to fret about the freeze-and-thaw cycles and deal with a lack of snow cover for part of the winter, occasionally garlic rots in raised beds, due to the lack of a huge volume of insulating soil. I combat this by mulching my garlic with straw, and it usually helps a great deal.

If you choose to grow herbs in raised beds, be aware that you might be watering more often during heat waves. Raised beds tend to dry out more quickly than in-ground beds. Using that good old straw mulch I just mentioned will help to conserve soil moisture. You can also erect shade cloth over your garden, if needed. —SN

It's a good idea to protect garlic with mulch if you're planting it in a raised bed.

17

Can herbs be grown in a mixed perennial or annual bed?

You bet! Long gone are the days when the vegetables were in the veggie bed, the flowers in the flower bed, and herbs confined to a small corner near the kitchen.

It makes even more sense to mix things up when doing so increases the biodiversity of our gardens. Many herbs, if not all, have multiple functions in the garden beyond the uses we have for them once harvested. Herbs are important in companion planting, as they can be insectary plants attracting beneficial insects. Their chemical signatures can repel unwanted visitors too, hence the technique of planting chives (*Allium schoenoprasum*) and garlic chives beside your roses to ward off black spot fungus. Beyond those qualities, herbs can be part of the layers of a resilient garden, being ground covers, at middle height or on the upper deck, so to speak. Herbs provide habitat for welcome visitors from shelter to food, as well as being larval hosts for some insects.

In thinking of the design of a garden, herbs can add interesting colours, textures, and forms of foliage. They provide fragrance and are a tactile sensory experience. Besides all that, placing your herbs in among mixed beds can add whimsy and delight human visitors.

So yes, let's include them in our mixed perennial and annual beds, and not relegate them to a "working" part of the garden. The same considerations regarding suitability of sun exposure, soil, and moisture requirements are essential. Additionally, consider the growing habits of all the plants in the bed. Many herbs are good spreaders and will need the necessary space to grow. They also won't be as productive if they are constrained by space or overshadowed by other plants. Likewise, consider root systems, and, if any of your herbs have rhizomatic roots, consider planting them in the bed in containers sunk into the soil. We don't want those roots in amongst your prized ornamental plants. Mint, sweet woodruff (*Galium odoratum*), and thyme (*Thymus* spp.), not to mention Russian sage (*Salvia yangii*), are good examples of those that like to roam.

It is important to factor in requirements for harvesting. Culinary herbs that will be snipped repeatedly throughout the season need to be sited for easy access, and that includes the smallest and shortest all the way to the super-large ones such as lovage. There is no point in placing even such a large herb at the back of the garden where it is hard to get to. You simply won't bother, and that is a shame. Provide access points, such as paving stones, so that all herbs are get-at-able. Those herbs that are harvested for their roots, usually in spring or fall, will need sufficient space around them to be easily dug up and portions replaced. I am thinking of horseradish, but also echinacea (*Echinacea* spp.) and yarrow (*Achillea* spp.) and even the proverbial dandelion.

So, go for it. Get those culinary, medicinal, and spiritual herbs into any bed you can. You won't regret it. —JM

Lovage (left) and Russian sage (right) are herbs that could never be called diminutive! These perennials need their space.

What is an herb spiral?

The name is pretty self-explanatory, but the design is fascinating and worthy of a more detailed description. Yes, it's a garden bed shaped like a spiral, and, yes, you primarily grow herbs in it (although plants such as container varieties of squash, dwarf or semi-dwarf tomatoes, and lettuce can also thrive in spiral beds). Because of the bed's unique shape, your plants have all their individual needs met in one compact space. The upper part of the spiral is taller than the base of the spiral. The raised centre ensures that the whole bed has excellent drainage.

Herb spirals are usually constructed from materials such as stone, brick, pavers, and untreated wood. The types of materials you use can render the bed as formal or informal as you like; a quick search online will yield some inspiring designs, from very rustic to clean and elegant. Some designs even incorporate ponds into the base!

To create the spiral, first ensure that the site you are using is in full sun (six or more hours per day), as most herbs prefer full sun. Clear the site of weeds, including turfgrass. While you can make your spiral any size you want, a typical diameter for the base is six feet (two metres). Continue laying your construction materials in a spiral shape, working from the outside into the middle. The end of the spiral should exit facing north, as water runs clockwise in the northern hemisphere. Stack the materials higher for each section of the spiral. The top of the spiral is usually about three feet (one metre) tall. You don't want it to be too tall or you won't be able to work with the bed—harvesting herbs while standing on a ladder isn't a fun prospect! As you build the layers, add growing medium. A mix of topsoil and compost is suitable.

In addition to being aesthetically pleasing, an herb spiral allows gardeners to grow herbs that love the sun the most—for example, oregano (*Origanum vulgare*), French tarragon (*Artemisia dracunculus* 'Sativa'), and basil—on the sunnier sides of the spiral, where they will receive abundant rays. Other herbs, such as rosemary, parsley (*Petroselinum* spp.), thyme, chives, and cilantro, can be tucked into less sunny areas.[3] —SN

20

The unique design of an herb spiral makes it an ideal structure to use with your herb plants.

Planting and Propagating Herbs

What is the difference between perennial (and biennial) and annual herbs?

It's all about the length of the life cycle! Annual herbs go through their entire life cycle in one growing season. That means you pop a seed in the ground in the spring, and the plant grows, flowers, and produces seed before the snow flies and the plant dies. Some annuals will reseed (I'm looking at you, borage!), so it can be a bit confusing when you spot them again in your garden the following year. Annual herbs include basil, cilantro, chervil (*Anthriscus cerefolium*), summer savory (*Satureja hortensis*), and anise (*Pimpinella anisum*). Some varieties of dill are annual as well.

Biennial herbs run through their life cycles in two years. During the first year, they focus on seed germination, and root and leaf formation. They will go dormant over the winter, then reappear the next spring. In the second year, they flower and set seed. Parsley is technically a biennial, although we tend to grow it as an annual on the prairies. Some dill varieties are biennial. Stevia (*Stevia rebaudiana*) is considered a biennial, but it's too cold here to overwinter outdoors, so we grow it as an annual.

Perennial herbs are those that come back year after year. (They don't live forever, though—each one has a particular lifespan.) What may be perennial in warmer climates may not survive over the winter in our hardiness zones, so watch your plant labels carefully. These include bay laurel, rosemary, fennel, lemongrass (*Cymbopogon* spp.), scented geranium (*Pelargonium* spp.), and cumin (*Cuminum cyminum*). Perennial herbs that can handle our winters include mint, tarragon, thyme, chives, some varieties of lavender, some varieties of sage (*Salvia* spp.), and oregano.[1]—SN

Oregano is a staple of many international dishes. If you don't eat it, the flowers are delicate and pretty. It's worth planting any way you choose to enjoy it!

I am ordering herb "plugs" from a supplier. What are plugs, and are there any special instructions for planting them?

The availability of plant plugs eliminates the need for a gardener to start seeds and grow out their own seedlings. A plug is a clump of growing medium containing a small seedling that has been grown from seed in the cell of a plug tray. The plants are sold in the trays that they are grown in once their roots are big enough to withstand the rigours of transplanting.

There are several benefits to purchasing plugs. The plants are young, which generally keeps the cost down for the consumer. The grower doesn't have to spend a lot of time raising the plants and spending money on inputs such as water and fertilizer. You might be familiar with annual (bedding) flower plants being sold this way, but it's also a common way to purchase small vegetables and herbs. The shape of the cells in the trays makes for an easier transplant when the seedlings are gently removed from the tray, as the growing medium surrounds and protects the plant roots. Many gardeners find that plugs are an economical way to purchase plants in bulk.

When they arrive, trays of plugs may be on the dry side. Give them a good drink a couple of hours before transplanting; don't plant them dry. When it's time to plant, ease the plugs out of their containers, being careful not to grab them too tightly by the stems as that can injure them. It is usually sufficient simply to give each cell a bit of a squeeze at the bottom to pop the plant out. Plant the plugs into containers or beds, but not too deeply! They need to be positioned at the same level as their original depth in the cell. Keep up with the watering, as needed. Don't fertilize your newly planted plugs right away; give them at least a week to settle in. (Check page 46 for tips on how to fertilize young herb plants.)[2] —SN

Growing herbs from plugs is cost effective and rewarding.

How do I choose healthy herb plants when I'm shopping in the garden centre?

Herbs in pots for transplanting into the garden or containers are expensive. Our rule of thumb is to buy only those plants that cannot easily be grown from seed. I tend to direct my buying power to those herbs that either have a low germination rate from seed or take a long time to grow to a useful size.

Before I buy, I want to choose herbs that are small, both in pot size and plant size, as they will settle in more readily after planting and be more productive that season. Hopefully, they are smaller in price, too!

Then I look for ones that are healthy. Which means I want to check their roots. Are they planted in soil that is bone dry, indicating potential root damage, or do they have roots growing out of the bottom of the pot, indicating that they are root-bound? If not, then I will gently lift the pot off the root ball and see if the roots are white and plump, meaning that they are in great shape. If they are tan and brittle, they are obviously damaged. Also, check if the roots are nicely spread through the soil or circling round and round, which should be avoided. That means they are root-bound, and will need to be loosened and spread out before planting to ensure the plant grows healthily.

I also check to see if the plant has been grown from a cutting, that the plug has been well planted, and it is not sticking up out of the soil, which will require special care when transplanting to ensure the plug is below soil level.

Next, check for signs and symptoms of pests or diseases. Is there any sign of mould on the soil? Are there lots of weeds growing in the medium? Does the plant appear wilted or discoloured, or have areas of necrosis where parts are brittle, or have damp spots with a sticky, slimy, or fuzzy coating? Are the leaves a nice colour with no signs of insect debris or holes from being chomped? If the leaves look healthy, we are onto a good thing.

Finally, I check my list and my wallet, and naturally succumb to that lovely herb plant calling my name. —JM

How do I get my soil into tip-top shape for a successful in-ground herb garden?

If you have perused our book *The Prairie Gardener's Go-To for Soil*, you'll know that there is a running theme throughout: organic matter is lovely stuff! Adding something as simple as compost can help improve your soil's structure and texture, combat compaction, and increase porosity and water-holding capacity. Not to mention, it gives all of the organisms living in the soil something to chow down on and work toward making your soil even better.

Don't till your soil (or, if you do, only scratch the surface) if you want to maintain healthy, living soil organisms and preserve soil structure. Reduced (or a lack of) tillage can also prevent weed seeds from breaking the surface of the soil and obtaining the sunlight, oxygen, and water needed to germinate.

If you have annual weeds in your herb garden, pick them while they are young, before they flower and set seed. You can just leave them on the surface of the soil where they will decompose and cycle back into the ground as compost. In that same vein, use the chop-and-drop method with cover crops. If you are growing annual herb plants and have harvested (or brought them indoors) before winter has set in, sow the seeds of a crop such as fall rye (*Secale cereale*) or field peas (*Pisum sativum*). The young plants can be cut down in spring and left in your garden bed to break down over the growing season. Your herb plants can be planted around them and reap the rewards of the extra nutrients. —SN

This exuberantly planted herb bed in a community garden holds a wealth of different herbs.

How do I sow herb seeds?

Growing herbs from seeds is the most economical and easiest way to get a lot of herbs. Not only that, but you get to choose from a huge array of species, varieties, and cultivars. Plus, you get to experience the joy of seeing those tiny seeds germinate!

We have choices about where, when, and how to sow our herb seeds. We can simply let them self-sow where they are in the garden and let whichever germinate do so. Certainly, this is the easiest method, as no work is involved at all. We can sow our seeds indoors under grow lights to become seedlings that we transplant later. We can sow seeds in containers that live outside over the winter and germinate when conditions are right. We can also direct sow or broadcast seeds in the spring in the garden bed or in containers.

We have discussed general direct sowing and indoor growing techniques in *The Prairie Gardener's Go-To for Seeds*, so we are confining ourselves to some specific tips for herbs here.

To begin, choose the easiest method of sowing for the species. For example, why grow dill indoors for transplanting outside when you can just let it self-sow or you can direct sow the seed? Semi-shrub herbs such as lavender and thyme are best sown indoors to be planted as seedlings.

These healthy basil seedlings are being grown indoors under lights.

Secondly, select your varieties and cultivars keeping in mind the time they will need to germinate and mature. Those with long germination periods such as parsley or garlic chives are best sown indoors given our shorter growing season. Dill, cilantro, and basil are our fastest-growing herbs so can be easily direct sown outdoors.

Be cognizant of any requirements for breaking dormancy beyond the usual criteria for moisture, air, soil temperature, and length of daylight. Some herbs have better germination if they are presoaked for up to twenty-four hours. These are mostly in the Apiaceae family, such as parsley and cilantro, or any others that have a harder than usual aril (outer shell).

Light versus darkness is another consideration. Most herb seeds are tiny and should be sown shallowly, with only a thin layer of growing medium to cover them and prevent them from drying out. Some are fussier. For instance, catnip (*Nepeta cataria*), thyme, and lemon balm should not be covered at all as they need light, but Johnny-jump-up or heartsease (*Viola tricolor*) require darkness.

Many of our herb seeds require stratification (exposure to cold temperatures for a period of time) before they will successfully germinate. My rule of thumb is that if an herb is perennial in nature, then it requires cold stratification, unless its native range is in the tropics. A few of the many that need to be stratified include anise hyssop (*Agastache foeniculum*), arnica (*Arnica* spp.), rosemary, and sage. There are a few herbs that need to be scarified, including marsh mallow (*Althaea* spp.)

When sowing, it pays dividends to pre-moisten the growing medium beforehand, then gently press seeds, spaced appropriately, into the medium, before sifting on top a bit more medium so that the seeds are at the correct depth. The temptation to sow too many seeds too closely together is almost overwhelming with herbs.

If I am sowing herb seeds indoors, I use a heating mat to keep the growing medium warm enough for good germination. I also use a capillary mat for bottom watering so that the soil stays evenly moist, and a dome over the tray to moderate humidity. But I also check regularly to ensure that the medium isn't too moist, and that humidity is not too high, to avoid problems. If I am direct sowing into containers or in a garden bed, I will cover the seeds with a floating row cover or use a cold frame to promote good germination and early growth.[3] —JM

31

How can I save the seeds from my herb plants?

Saving my herb seeds is one of my seasonal delights! I have mounds of calendula, dill, and cilantro/coriander seeds that are all packaged up for sowing next year. These three are easy ones—annual herbs that have tons of seeds to start your herb seed–saving addiction off nicely. But don't stop there, as our biennial and perennial herb seeds are perfectly within our grasp.

Saving herb seeds starts with allowing a plant to flower (yes, you actually get to enjoy the flowers, as do the insects). It means forgoing harvesting more of the leaves, as the goal is to allow the plant to divert its energy from growing leaves to producing flowers, and then, after being fertilized, having the seeds mature on the plant. In the end, the plants look dreadful for the most part, as we are letting them complete their growing cycle for the season as their foliage dries out and their seed heads become dry and tan coloured.

The trick is to allow the plants to stand for as long as is necessary for the seeds to mature on the plant. I often allow the first stems of flowers to be the ones that I designate as being for seed, so that they have the longest possible time to mature before the first frost arrives. The rest are kept flower-free so I can harvest the leaves. Before you decide that it is time to harvest, inspect the seed heads. The seeds inside will be tan, brown, or black. If they are skinny, white, or green and just look unfinished, then they are, and there is no use collecting them.

The goal is to collect the seeds before they spill onto the ground. Sometimes I enclose a seed head or heads in a paper or muslin bag so that I don't lose my harvest. Borage is one herb that I always missed until I started using the bags. Others like calendula and dill stay intact long enough to be snipped off and placed in my bucket. Still others that are enclosed in tough shells, like poppy (*Papaver* spp.), can be collected by placing a large paper envelope beneath the seed head and gently shaking it or bending it over, which will allow you to collect the seeds. Occasionally, if it is getting late in the season, I will pull the entire plant out, or snip it down to the crown if perennial, and place it in a big paper bag in the hope that the seeds will get a bit more maturing time.

Do not shut up any container with freshly collected seeds as they still contain moisture that needs to evaporate from the seeds. Doing so will almost definitely result in mould growing on the seeds, rendering them useless.

After seeds are thoroughly dry, clean them by removing chaff and other debris before placing them in envelopes or other containers for storage.[4] —JM

Calendula's dry seeds make them easy to collect. (And they also fall off the plant with excessive ease, often providing volunteer plants the following year.)

How do I store seeds from my herb plants to plant next year?

The key to successful seed storage is simple: your seeds must be dry to begin with, and they need to stay dry. Store them in glass or plastic jars, or in envelopes made of regular or glassine paper. Label them carefully with the name of the plant and the date they were harvested. Keep them in a dry place and you'll be good to go for next year (and most likely they will remain viable beyond that!). Storing seeds in the refrigerator can introduce moisture that you don't want, as well as subject them to fluctuating temperatures as the fridge door opens and closes frequently. Storage in the freezer can be done if you're looking to store seeds for a very long time, but again, watch those changing temperatures when you reach for the ice cream!—SN

The beautiful comas (fluffy parachutes) of milkweed seeds are easy to grasp when harvesting. Make sure all of the seeds are perfectly dry before you store them.

How can I propagate herbs via cuttings?

Stem cuttings can be taken from side shoots that have at least two sets of leaves, not from the main stem of a plant. Look for ones that haven't yet developed flower buds, and preferably recent growth, not those that have become "woody." You also want to take cuttings when plants are actively growing (spring), rather than when they are entering dormancy (fall). Then, with a sharp knife, slice off the shoot just below a leaf node. This is where the active growing point of the stem is located. You can cut the stem shorter but do ensure you have two to four inches (five to ten centimetres) of stem to work with plus that node. Of course, some plants, such as basil, will grow adventitious roots at any point on the stem once in water. If possible, cut the end of the stem at an angle to increase the surface area for rooting to occur. Be sure to take more cuttings than you think you will need, because not all cuttings will take.

Now comes the decision of whether to root the cuttings in water or in a soilless growing medium. Rooting occurs quickly in water; slower in a growing medium.

Herbs that root well in water include basil, most mints, lemon verbena (*Aloysia citriodora*), and rosemary, but I have had success with many others. Conventionally, more herbs do best in a growing medium and these include bay laurel, catnip, tarragon, oregano, hyssop (*Hyssopus officinalis*), lavender, mints, sage, southernwood (*Artemisia abrotanum*), and winter savory (*Satureja montana*). Should you choose to root your cuttings in water, be sure to change the water frequently to prevent bacterial growth. Do pot them as soon as they have developed ½-inch (1.25-centimetre) roots, making sure to pat the soil all around the stem so that there is good contact. If a cutting has been grown in water for too long, it rarely seems to like being transferred to a growing medium as the roots have adapted to the watery medium.

Those cuttings that are trying to root in a growing medium have a rougher time, so you will need to give them some TLC. You have the option to dip the roots in a rooting hormone, which will stimulate faster growth. Place in a pre-moistened growing medium, ensuring that the stem is in good contact with the medium. The cuttings should be able to stand up by themselves. They have little access to water until roots form, so they must absorb moisture through their leaves. Spray or mist them frequently. You can also use a much-diluted liquid seaweed fertilizer, which helps to promote root formation. Cover the pot or tray with a simple plastic bag or humidity dome to trap humidity inside. This helps keep the stems hydrated.

You will know when your cuttings have rooted well when a gentle tug on the stem doesn't dislodge them. If new leaves are forming, you can really celebrate. At this point, you can pot each cutting into larger individual pots.[5] —JM

Look at those fabulous roots! These basil plants have been rooted in water and are ready to transplant.

Can herbs be propagated by layering? Which ones?

Layering is a simple method to grow more plants from a stem, while it is still attached to a mother plant. You can layer many of the perennial herbs you are growing outdoors, and the same procedure works for many herbs that you have potted up for indoors. Mint, thyme, catnip, catmint, sage, and rosemary are all good candidates for layering. To layer your herb plants, follow these steps:

1. Carefully bend a healthy stem to the ground. Remove the leaves from the middle and lower part of the stem, the part that you've bent. There should be leaves on the top six inches (fifteen centimetres) of the plant.
2. Cover the now leafless bent part of the stem with soil. If the stem refuses to stay in place, you can gently peg it down with a landscape staple. The leafy part of the top of the plant should be sticking up into the air.
3. Water the plant and ensure it is watered regularly as it grows new roots.
4. After a few weeks, the new plant will have roots and you can cut it away from the mother plant.[6] — SN

Catmint delightfully reseeds itself with enthusiasm, and it can be easily divided, but layering is yet another great option for its propagation.

How do I go about dividing perennial herbs?

Division is an efficient and effective method to increase your stock of herbs, not to mention it will provide you with many to share with your fellow herb enthusiasts. Perennial herbs can be divided either in early fall or mid-spring, depending on the weather and the stage of growth. Avoid dividing them when they are in full leaf production, as the operation will necessarily mean the new divisions will spend more time on root growth than leaf growth for some time after the operation.

Before dividing any perennial herb, water it well for a couple of days beforehand so that the plant is well hydrated. The soil will be softer too, making it easier to do the necessary digging and hopefully reduce root damage. Remove any weeds that you can see growing in or around the plant. Do harvest at least one-third of the foliage to start with, which will reduce the stress on the plant after it is divided, for it won't need as much water. It will also make it easier to see how far from the crown you will need to dig to keep most of the roots intact as well as where the natural divisions in the clump are occurring.

Lay down a tarp beside where you are working, as well as a tub with some water nearby so you can put the herb plants into water as soon as they are divided. Then, using a sharp transplant spade (it is narrower and has the same width all the way down as well as a gentler curve at the bottom, which allows for precise digging), dig all around the plant first, down to the depth of the root ball, then gently lever up the entire plant to place on the tarp. Those herbs with either deep taproots or large fleshy roots that you are not able to completely remove from the soil may need to have some roots sliced off with a sharp knife once you get deep enough to remove a good chunk of the root for dividing.

Most herbs that can be divided fall into a few groups. On one side are those that you can easily separate by gently pulling them apart. Chives and garlic chives are composed of individual bulbs, and all you need to do is pull off a dozen or so to form a decent-sized division. Those that form mats with shallow fibrous roots or adventitious roots growing wherever the stems meet the soil can also be pulled apart into sections. Just make sure you have a stem or two attached to each handful of roots. Thyme and sweet woodruff are perfect examples. Many others such as oregano and lemongrass also have shallow, fibrous roots that can be pulled apart or cut easily into pieces.

Those with rhizomes such as mint or underground roots like bee balm (*Monarda* spp.) can be divided by carefully extracting any roots that have migrated away from the mother plant. Often these extra roots, gathered together, can have enough mass to be planted together for a new plant. This technique also has the benefit of keeping the mother plant within bounds and remaining vigorous. You can also dig up the mother plant and unwind and pull apart sections of roots to make many more plants.

A sharp knife is necessary to help divide herbs plants that have tap, woody, or fleshy roots. When the plant is out on the tarp, look for sections that, once sliced off, will have a large piece of root as well as one or more stems arising from the root. Taprooted herbs include many in the carrot family, such as lovage, stinging nettle and angelica (*Angelica* spp.), that are perennial to our climate. Fleshy-rooted herbs include horseradish and comfrey (*Symphytum* spp.), and both come with the caveat that if you divide them, chances are that the original site will grow another plant as it is almost impossible to get all the root pieces unearthed. Peony (*Paeonia* spp.) is another fleshy-rooted herb that occasionally will regrow in its original site. Woody or semi-shrub herbs I avoid dividing, as often their roots are brittle. I give those herbs lots of space when originally planting them and leave them be. Lavender is a great example of a woody-rooted herb, and if we are lucky enough to have it survive for a few winters, we shouldn't do anything to endanger it!

Those herb divisions that you wish to replant in the garden should be planted immediately to avoid undue stress on them. Divisions that are to go elsewhere should be potted up as soon as possible in moist potting soil. When replanting divisions, there is no need to amend the garden soil. Simply transplant the division into the soil, keeping the crown at the same height as it was in the original medium. Then add a layer of compost about 1 inch (2.5 centimetres) thick. There is no need for fertilizers at this point as the herb will be seeking to repair its root system first, before resuming growth. Water well, but not to the point of saturating the soil, and provide protection from heat and the sun.[7] —JM

Growing and
Cultivating Herbs

3

How do I know when it's time to water my herb plants?

Not all herbs have the same watering requirements, but for the most part, they're going to let you know in similar ways when they need a drink. Often, they'll wilt to show their displeasure. Sometimes the leaves will turn yellow in colour. Bear in mind, however, that these signs can also indicate other problems—such as overwatering or a nutrient deficiency. The only way to truly know if plants are needing water is to test the growing medium. Stick a finger up to the second knuckle into the growing medium (or, if you have enough room to do so, use a garden trowel and sink it up to the top of the blade). If you don't feel any moisture or the trowel doesn't have any damp medium clinging to it when you pull it out, watering is likely in order.

If your herbs are in a hot, windy spot or in a full-sun location, check them frequently as they may need more irrigation. Container-grown herbs have a smaller volume of growing medium to live in than those in ground or in a raised bed, so they may dry out more quickly. As well, the more intensively (closely together) you've spaced your herb plants, the more competitive they may be for water. There is a seasonal component to watering your outdoor-grown herb plants, as well. Spring on the prairies is often wetter and colder than the rest of the growing season, so your plants won't necessarily need supplemental watering. Likewise, in the autumn, a perennial herb's watering requirements will slow down with the cooler weather and the oncoming dormancy period. One general rule to follow: whether you're growing herbs indoors or out, you'll want to ensure that you're not giving them boggy soil to sit and rot in. Water them only when they need it.[1] —SN

Wild bergamot (Monarda fistulosa) *is quite tolerant of dry conditions,
but it will still welcome some help with irrigation during periods of
prolonged drought.*

When is the best time of day to water my herb plants?

Herbs, like most plants, thrive when they receive moisture during the earlier part of the day. It doesn't necessarily mean you need to be up at dawn, though watering as the sun rises is a great way to start the day off!

The reasons are manifold. When temperatures are cool, the water applied has a chance to percolate through the soil profile to reach the root zone. Less water is lost to evaporation as the day's heat builds, so all that you apply goes to where it is supposed to go. When plants have access to ample moisture, they are well hydrated and have maximum turgidity. The result is that they are under less stress, even during the heat of the day. Additionally, the leaves will have plentiful amounts of aromatic oils, which give them their great taste and fragrance.

Ideal timing aside, I always maintain that if you cannot get out early in the day, then whenever you can get out is best so that your plants do not fry for lack of moisture! —JM

If it's possible, water before the sun gets too high in the sky.

What is the best fertilizer to use with herb plants?

Most herbs don't need an extremely fertile growing medium; in fact, too much succulent fresh growth can invite pests and diseases and sometimes wreaks havoc with the volatile oil content in an herb plant's parts. (As the oils are often the reason you are harvesting the plant, they yield properties such as fragrance and flavour. You'll want to make sure your growing medium isn't too rich, especially in nitrogen.) If you're growing herbs such as mint, thyme, oregano, tarragon, or rosemary, using a lean growing medium is preferable.

Whether you are growing herbs in containers or in garden beds, amendments of compost or vermicompost (worm castings) in the spring are suitable. Although we cannot measure the exact ratio of nutrients contained in compost (every shovelful is different!), plants still benefit from the slow release of some of these nutrients over the growing season.

If you're agreeable to using a synthetic fertilizer, there are many on the market that are formulated for herbs. These products are not slow release, and you will know from the packaging the exact percentage of macronutrients they contain. If you choose to use them, be aware that more is not better. They can severely burn plants if too much is applied. Follow the recommended rate of application on the package. If the plants are young, dilute the concentration by at least one-half.[2] —SN

Tarragon is low maintenance to begin with, and on top of that, you don't need to fertilize it very often. Our kind of herb plant!

What does it mean to "pinch back" herbs? Why and when should we do this?

Pinching back herbs should occur early in the season. It is a form of pruning, but it is performed just as the plant really gets going. The goal is to encourage side branching of stems, and thus more leaf production for our favourite herbs.

When pinching back, plants should be at the juvenile stage, when they have at least two sets of true leaves. I usually wait until I see the third set before acting. Then, using your fingernails or a sharp pair of mini-snippers, snip off the third set of leaves and the stalk back to the second set, as close to the node as possible, but try to avoid damaging the dormant buds in the leaf axils. Removing that third set of leaves and stalk prompts the plant to grow at least two side stalks from the node. Plants contain a hormone, auxin, which acts to suppress side growth. Removing that top set of leaves removes the auxin so that side branching can happen.

Once the plant has developed a couple more sets of leaves on the new stalks, then repeat the action. You can pinch back multiple times to get lots of side branching, but stop by early summer to let the plants take off. And, of course, use the snippings for your dinner so they don't go to waste!

Herbs with woody stems should not be pinched back by more than one-third at a time.

You can pinch back later in the season, if the plants are getting too leggy or if the stems are becoming too fibrous and you would prefer softer stalks and younger leaves with generally a milder taste.

Many herbs respond well to pinching back, especially those in the mint family. Basil, lavender, oregano, rosemary, sage, and thyme also react very well to this cultural practice.[3] —JM

Lavender responds well to pinching back and will reward you with fresh new growth.

Are there any herbs that are aggressive spreaders in the garden? What can I do to control them if I want to plant them?

Most of the herbs we grow in our prairie gardens are grown as annuals, so we don't have to worry too much about aggressively spreading perennials. The biggest culprit—which just so happens to be a much-desired herb that many of us are keen on planting—is mint. In an in-ground or a raised bed, a single seemingly innocent little mint plant can wreak all sorts of havoc. Underground, mint is a beast, spreading quickly via rhizomes. Even in our cold climate, mint can take over sizable real estate in a few short growing seasons. When you go to dig it out, it can prove to be a nearly impossible task. A well-meaning gardener planted it in an in-ground bed in a community garden I belonged to and when we went to "tame it" a few years later, the rhizomes were as thick as my thumb and had travelled in all directions from the main plant. Some of them were several feet away!

To keep mint under control, plant it in a large container, and sink the container into the ground. A plastic container is usually the best as it can withstand being in the ground over successive seasons. In this way, the rhizomes are corralled, and the plant can still be happy outdoors. After a few years, you'll have to dig the container up and divide the plant as it will have filled up the available space in the pot and will likely be showing some signs of decline because of this. (Yellowing leaves, wilting, requiring more water than it used to, and dying out in the centre of the plant are all possible indicators that division is in order.)

A couple of other perennial herbs that can be a bit problematic due to their propensity to rigorously self-seed are lovage and chives. I'm of the opinion that chives belong to the "the more, the merrier" club, but I know many people who don't share my enthusiasm for them and want to manage only one tidy clump. To do this, deadhead the flowers before they set seed. The same goes for lovage: trim those lovely umbels off before they set seed, and you'll be able to successfully wrangle this fascinating—and tasty—member of the celery family. Fortunately, both plants have seedlings that are extremely easy to recognize, so if you miss a few seeds and they germinate, you can pull the volunteers (and eat them!) long before they mature. —SN

Some gardeners find the propensity of chives to self-seed to be irritating, but if you're a fan of this pretty herb, you'll want to hang on to a few plants for the pollinators and to add flavour to your cooking. Did you know that you can make delicious vinegars and jellies with the blossoms?

Do I need to deadhead the flowers of my herb plants? How should I do it?

We usually deadhead or remove the flowers from our ornamental plants once they have finished blooming and before they start to set seed. The action not only makes the plants neat and tidy but may prompt them to have a further flush of flowers.

With herbs we want to deadhead the flowers before they form or at the very least as they open. It seems a shame to remove their flowers but doing so prevents the plant from completing its life cycle so that it will grow more leaves for our use. Not only that, but many herbs' taste will change once they flower, usually becoming more bitter.

Of course, if you want to collect seeds from a plant, you will need to let it flower and set seed as soon as possible, given our shortish growing season. The other reasons for letting an herb plant flower are to attract beneficial insects and provide food for wildlife. If flowers, immature flowers, or dried seeds are the objective, we need to let those herbs flower and set seed before deadheading. Borage, calendula, catmint (*Nepeta* spp.), German chamomile (*Matricaria recutita*), chives, cilantro, dill, echinacea, lavender, and yarrow are just a few to let flower. Some herbs, of course, are prolific, so if you do not want a lot of volunteer plants, then nip them in the bud and deadhead them.

It is easy to deadhead herbs. Snip stalks right back to the next node as soon as you see a flower stalk shooting up. Simply nip them off with your fingernails or use a pair of sharp snippers to do the job. The trick is to remove the flower bud back to the next set of leaves, which will encourage further branching and leave the plant looking well kept instead of a bunch of stalks sticking out of the plant like a hedgehog.[4]—JM

If you want to have seeds, flowers are a must! These sage plants will eventually be harvested for seeds.

My herb plants have gone to seed too quickly! What causes this and what can I do about it?

The key phrase here is "too quickly." It's important to recognize that flowering and going to seed are natural parts of the life cycle of most plants—they need to reproduce! When a plant starts entering its sexual reproductive phase too early in its life cycle, it is called bolting. Bolting usually occurs as a response to some sort of stressor, such as a sudden increase (or, for some plants, decrease) in temperature, a lack of water or nutrients, or even an overexposure to sunlight. When under extreme stress, plants perceive that they might not survive and move quickly to produce a new generation. As gardeners, we usually don't want our herb plants to bolt—we would prefer that they live out their full life cycles uninterrupted by trauma and drama. There is the added problem that some herbs, such as cilantro, chervil, and tarragon, tend to become unpalatable once they've bolted, rendering them useless as culinary herbs. Fortunately, there are a few things we can do to prevent or slow bolting.

Once the green seeds of cilantro are fully formed and dried, they can be harvested as coriander spice. What a versatile plant!

1. Don't site your plants in the wrong spot. That seems logical, but if you have limited space, you might try to push the envelope a little. Research the sunlight requirements of your herb plants, and don't park a lover of dappled shade into full baking sun.
2. Minimize drought stress by providing supplemental irrigation when required. Add mulch to help conserve soil moisture.
3. If your region is under a heat wave, it might be helpful to move your herb plants into a more sheltered location away from unrelenting, blazing heat.
4. Ensure the plant's nutritional needs are met, especially if you are growing your herbs in containers, where nutrients are quickly used up. (See page 46 for tips on how to give your plants a proper nutritional boost.)
5. Don't let your herb plants flower. Trim off the blooms as soon as you spot them.

One thing to remember: if you're saving seeds (and hopefully you are!), it's not the end of the world if your herb plants bolt, because you'll at least be able to grow out their progeny.[5] —SN

Can I eat my culinary herb plants after they have flowered?

It depends! If you're growing chives, you're probably eating the leaves and flowers at the same time for most of the season, and not only are both plant parts delicious, but the plant is unaffected by the harvests. It is important to consider that herbs that produce flowers have done so by redirecting energy that they would usually put into producing tasty leaves, so the bright flavour of the leaves may be slightly diminished with herbs such as basil, nasturtium, mint, thyme, oregano, and marjoram. Other herbs such as cilantro, watercress, sorrel, and tarragon can become bitter after they have been allowed to flower and their leaf and stem textures may be altered as well.[6] —SN

Can I sow herb seeds in the fall so that they grow the following spring?

Absolutely! I always take my cue from the garden. If I reliably see seeds germinating in early spring that must have dropped the previous fall, then I know that I am onto a good thing. For instance, I have a little corner of an herb bed in my home garden where I have given up on planting any tender herbs. It is always a riot of chives, borage, calendula, poppy, viola, and dill that I never, ever deliberately sow.

The best herbs to sow in fall are the annual and biennial species, with a caveat that they need to be hardy to our climate. Simply let them fall and lie on the surface of the soil as you are clearing the plant debris, and they will germinate come spring when conditions for breaking dormancy are fulfilled. Any that get buried a bit deeper in the soil through cultivation will emerge a little later and be a second crop for late summer or early fall. There is a wide array of species beyond the ones already mentioned, such as anise hyssop, chervil, cilantro, and chamomile, that are great for sowing. In fact, I have so much cilantro seed in my community garden bed, I am having to either pot extras up to give them away or weed the excess seedlings out each spring!

Biennial species for fall sowing include forget-me-not (*Myosotis* spp.), foxglove (*Digitalis* spp.), and flat-leaved and curly parsley. Generally, I want to be more intentional as to where these herbs pop up, for ease of both harvesting and care. In particular, foxglove should be sited away from curious fingers due to its toxins. A word to the wise about forget-me-not, as well: it loves to spread everywhere, so vigorous culling is required.

Perennial herbs that love to self-sow include bee balm, chives, garlic chives, lovage, horseradish, monkshood, oregano, sage, stinging nettle, thyme, and tarragon. Perennials often have a lower rate of germination and have fewer seeds, so you may not experience the same rate of success. The exception is lovage. If you forget to deadhead regularly or if you let the seeds mature for the birds to eat over the winter, you may have a bumper crop of seedlings next spring.

Beyond these stalwarts, experiment with other herb plants as you never know what will happen. I cheered the spring that my fall-sown basil popped up and provided me with a plentiful crop that summer. — JM

Cilantro will readily pop up nice and fresh in the spring if you sow the seeds in the previous autumn.

How should I prepare my perennial herbs for winter?

Our hardy and many half-hardy herbs can overwinter very nicely in our gardens, thank you very much. The first step I always take come fall is to determine which ones are to stay behind and which are coming inside for the winter, given that there really isn't space for everyone in the house. Not only that, but many of our hardy herbs want and need a long winter's sleep.

Part of deciding which half-hardy herbs get left behind is to evaluate if they can survive our winter's weather. For example, I wouldn't have left common oregano outside ten years ago, but now it overwinters beautifully. Then I make sure to harvest any remaining leaves and seeds. They really get a good haircut, right down to the crown.

Some varieties of thyme will successfully overwinter on the prairies.

Then I tease out or remove any weeds that have been lurking in or around the plants, and I check to make sure that they are all within their boundaries and not migrating into each other. Then I divide them if needed. (See pages 38–39 for more detail on that operation.) I will also take the time to add any soil amendments or fertilizers that might be desired, lightly scratching them into the soil.

Next up is to ensure that there is around 1 to 2 inches (2.5 to 5 centimetres) of mulch all around the plants, but not encroaching on their crowns. This is an essential step for any herbs that are newly planted or have been recently divided, and even any that were planted in the current year, as their roots will more readily suffer damage with freeze-and-thaw cycles.

Should I be wanting to test my luck on winter herb hardiness, those plants in question may get a little extra treatment in the form of an additional layer of mulch around them (but not on top), and, if I am really chancing my luck with some plants, perhaps some floating row cover to provide a bit of extra protection. Alternatively, for these herbs I might deploy a portable cold frame to fit right overtop of them.

Finally, just before the soil really gets down to business of freezing solid, the plants get a careful watering. Then it is up to them to weather our winter weather, and we get the fun come spring of greeting their new growth! —JM

Which herbs can I successfully overwinter indoors?

Perennial herbs such as lovage, Russian tarragon (*Artemisia dracunculus*), chives, thyme, and mint can be left outdoors, cozily surrounded by mulch, until they reawaken in the spring. Sometimes biennial herbs that we usually treat as annuals, such as parsley, might also have a chance at weathering the cold of our extreme climate, so it might be worth experimenting and leaving them in the ground. Annual herbs need to be brought indoors if you intend to try to keep growing them; these include basil, nasturtium, cilantro, stevia, and dill.

One way to overwinter your annual herbs is by taking cuttings (see pages 35–36 for instructions on how to do this). If you're worried that your parsley might not survive the winter elements or you just want to pot up a plant for your indoor kitchen garden, take cuttings from it, as well. The same goes for your perennial herbs—if you want mint for your mojitos in the dead of January, take cuttings from your outdoor mint plants before you put the garden to bed during the previous autumn. Basil is another good candidate for cuttings, as it doesn't respond well to transplanting from an in-ground or raised bed.

Another option is to bring the actual plants indoors for the winter. This might not be a good idea if your plants are large, but you might be able to divide them into smaller chunks when you dig them up. If you are growing your herbs in containers instead of in ground, you may be able to bring whole planters indoors. There are several things to watch out for, however. First and foremost, you don't want to drag pest insects into your house. After you have dug up the plants that you want to save, give them a good blast of water from the garden hose, ensuring that you've thoroughly sprayed all parts of the leaves and stems. Then carefully remove as much soil from the roots as you can without damaging the plants. Transplant them into fresh potting soil in clean containers. As an extra precaution, you can also quarantine them in a heated garage or other indoor area away from other plants you already have in the house.

The plants will need to be fully acclimatized to their new warm, dry environment to survive. You can achieve this by performing a reverse hardening-off process. Keep an eye on the long-range forecast and if things are looking a tad frosty over the next few weeks, start bringing the herb plants you want to save indoors every night. Take them back out during the day, and repeat these steps for at least two weeks, gradually increasing the number of hours they are indoors until they are ready to be inside full-time.

Ensure that the needs of your new indoor herb plants are being met: give them the proper amount of sunlight according to the type of plant they are, and water them when required (but definitely don't overdo it on the H_2O or you'll face rot and a whole host of potentially fatal problems). If you're unsure about what they like best, check the label that came with them or reference them in a seed catalogue. If you intend to harvest herb plants through the winter months, you may have to keep up with a regular fertilizing schedule. If you're focused on harvesting the lush, green leaves, you'll need a fertilizer with more nitrogen (the first number on the fertilizer packaging). Water-soluble fertilizers are suitable, and don't go full-strength: dilute them by at least half. Fertilize your herb "snowbirds" every two weeks. — SN

Stevia must be brought indoors to overwinter. We're just fine with that, as it means we can harvest it whenever we want a sweet herb to add to our hot tisanes.

I am so frustrated with trying to overwinter rosemary indoors. Are there any tips to help?

I don't know a single gardener who hasn't killed off a rosemary plant come February at least once. Overwintering rosemary used to be an oxymoron for me but no more!

The trick as always is to go back to a plant's roots and find out what weather it gets in its native habitat. Rosemary is a broadleaf evergreen. It is native to the Mediterranean, which has cool temperatures, lots of humidity, and lots of bright light in the winter.

Given that our homes are generally warm and dry with low light levels, the challenge is to give them what they need to survive and hopefully thrive till it is safe for them to go outside again.

Start by repotting the plants in a well-draining potting mix, such as that used for succulents and cacti, as soon as temperatures start to decline in early fall. Continue to leave the pot outside during the day so long as the temperatures are above 55°F (12°C) but bring it back in at night, so it can start to acclimatize to its new abode. Once it is time for it be indoors permanently, place it in bright light, preferably under grow lights, though a southwest-facing window is a good option, too. If the place is also on the cool side, that is a bonus, with daytime temperatures of 60 to 65°F (16 to 18°C) being best for the plant, though possibly on the chilly side for you.

Now comes the hard part. We tend to overwater to compensate for low humidity. Rosemary needs the opposite conditions, so provide the humidity by placing the pot on a pea gravel–filled tray topped up with water. As the water evaporates it will modify the humidity around the plant. Water only occasionally, when the soil has thoroughly dried out, as rosemary hates soggy soil. A few leaves may dry and drop off, but resist all temptation to increase watering!

You can also overwinter larger rosemary plants in unheated garages that have a nice bright window. Simply bring in an entire pot or two or repot the rosemary as above, and place near the light source. A floating row cover provides some insulation. Rosemary plants will hang out happily all winter with only a little water added occasionally.

Come spring, reverse the acclimatization process over a couple of weeks, taking the plants outside for gradually longer periods of time. You should be good to go for lots of new growth.[7] —JM

Rosemary can be a huge challenge to overwinter indoors, but it can be successfully done!

My lavender plants always die over the winter. How can I achieve better success with them?

There is no doubt about it. Growing lavender on the prairies is tricky. The Okanagan Valley in British Columbia is perfect for them, but then it is a plant hardiness zone or two better off for this most fragrant herb of all.[8]

Lavender originated around the Mediterranean Sea where it is hot, dry, and sunny. We get those conditions in the summer for sure; it is the winter that is the challenge.

But there is no need to throw in the trowel and call it a day.

What we need to do is select the absolute best site that can replicate those growing conditions and choose species, varieties, and cultivars that are the very hardiest of them all.

There are some forty-seven species in the lavender genus. Forget about Spanish lavender (*Lavandula stoechas*), French lavender (*L. pedunculata*), or even Egyptian lavender (*L. multifida)* unless you are looking for an annual plant or want to bring it inside for the winter.

We are looking for English lavender (*L. angustifolia*) and its various cultivars. Traditionally, two cultivars, 'Munstead' and 'Hidcote', named after famous English gardens, are recommended as being the hardiest of them all. Lavender is a sub-shrub, with a large and spreading root system once established. It is also a moderate grower, adding a few inches of stem and root growth a year as it matures. It is getting it to that point that is the goal.

Select a spot that has extremely well-draining soil, that is in as much sun and warmth as you can provide. Root rot is a concern as it hates having soggy roots. The lavender that I have grown for a number of years now is in a mounded bed about six inches (fifteen centimetres) high and bordered by rocks for additional warmth. (Another suggestion is to plant them close to a wall for the warmth that gives off.) My soil is actually on the lean side and a bit lower in organic matter than usual. It also doesn't get much in the way of snow cover, which I think is key to avoiding crown rot. The high pH in that part of the garden helps too as lavender prefers alkaline soils over acidic ones.

To encourage your lavender to establish quickly, water it regularly but avoid too much at a time. Once established they are really drought tolerant, so in the second year back off on the water a bit and by the third year they should be very resilient. Do mulch around the plants, but not deeply or at all close to the crown to avoid stem rot. An inch (2.5 centimetres) or so is good enough.

Lavender is meant to be an evergreen, but our harsh winters desiccate those leaves, so they can look pretty withered by spring. Avoid the temptation to hard prune the stems until spring is well under way and the plant has had a chance to recover from the winter, with new leaves growing in the axils of the stems. Once you know how far down the stem any winter dieback has gone, then it is time to prune. If we are lucky and it has been a mild winter, with no dieback, then prune approximately one-third of the stems to encourage bushiness and flowering.[9]

You can also grow lavender in pots and bring them inside for the winter, either stashing them in an unheated garage or directly inside after being repotted into fresh growing medium and quarantined for come-along-for-the-ride insect visitors. Be warned though: you need to provide the same growing conditions inside as out.

One last thing: lavender is not extremely long-lived. Ten years is about it, so when mine didn't come back one year I mourned it and its good life. Then I planted another one.

Are you up for the challenge? I always am! —JM

One of these types of lavender will overwinter in ground better than the other. Can you guess which one? If you said the 'Munstead' lavender on the right, you've got it! The plant on the left is Spanish lavender, which we have to treat as an annual on the prairies.

What are the dangers of growing and using herbs?

Herbs are powerful plants. They contain chemicals that have evolved over the aeons as defences against predators and pathogens. Similarly, they have properties that entice, smelling wonderful, so that they will be pollinated or protected by insects. Those properties mean that these plants are not to be taken lightly.

It behooves each and every one of us, as gardeners, to know the properties of our plants so we can safeguard ourselves if necessary. Some will irritate our skin if sap falls on it (phototoxic). Some will inject formic acid into our skin (stinging nettle), cause our eyes to water, and scratch us, in addition to other perils that come with growing them. A few are outright deadly to handle or ingest. Think foxglove (*Digitalis* spp.) and monkshood (*Aconitum* spp.), not to mention deadly nightshade (*Atropa belladonna*).

I am not an herbalist, by training or inclination, nor is Sheryl. We have a healthy respect for the myriad benefits of herbal preparations and remedies, but we never promote to others the health benefits, either preventive or restorative, of any of the herbs we grow. To use and misuse herbs can lead to many well-documented ill effects.[10] Yet I have used a comfrey leaf as a temporary bandage when I have scratched myself. I use calendula as a salve for my chapped hands after a day in the garden and I put lavender in my bath. We both drink scads of mint tisane and I swear by a nettle infusion for reducing inflammation.

We are careful not to eat too much sorrel or nasturtium leaves in our salads, for the properties of these salad herbs can upset our digestive systems. Nor would we prepare any remedies for others without the necessary training and consultation with medical professionals.

We don't want to scare anyone off growing herbs. Quite the contrary. It is the lore, mystique, and meaning of our herbs, along with the myriad of functions they have for us and our gardens, that make them so immensely satisfying to grow. But we do believe as gardeners that all plants demand our respect. After all, they evolved long before our species ever did, and we should always respect our elders![11] —JM

Sorrel is a wonderful culinary herb, but it should be enjoyed in moderation.

Harvesting and
Storing Herbs

4

How do I harvest my herbs?

The growth habits of your herbs dictate how you harvest them. Most herbs fall into either a branching structure with many shoots growing from a main stem or stems growing from a basal crown or directly from a rhizome.

To harvest those herbs that are growing from a branching plant, such as basil, oregano, or bay laurel, the goal is to clip, snip, or pinch a section of the shoot back to the next growing node, without leaving part of the internode (area on the stalk between growing points) waving in the breeze. Doing so will inhibit further growth, as the plant doesn't know what to do. The stalk just stays there until it dies back to the next growing point.

This method of harvesting is really pinching back but should be done on a mature plant, not a seedling. Harvest as much as you want but leave two-thirds of the plant behind so it has enough energy to keep on growing. If your plant is trying to flower, harvesting up to half of the plant will deter that tendency and promote further leafy growth for more harvests.

Those plants growing from their crowns include parsley, oregano, and echinacea, just to name a few. These herbs should be harvested by snipping back the leaves and stems to just above the crown. This action will promote further growth of shoots.

Herbs that have rhizomatic roots encompass lemongrass, mint, bee balm, and even ginger (*Zingiber officinale*) if you are growing it indoors. (Though if you are after its roots, you will want to dig up the entire ginger plant.) You want to cut the stems of these plants back to just above the rhizome, but leave a little nub, which will generate regrowth of the stem and also promote latent growth points on the rhizome. Mint is one herb that has both rhizomatic roots and a branching habit of growth. I prefer to snip each stem to the ground to keep the plant bushy and vigorous.

Herbs harvested for their flowers include lavender, borage, calendula, chamomile, and chives, to name a few. Flowers should be snipped or nipped off just after they have opened for maximum freshness. For those that are terminal flowers, nip off the entire flower just where it joins the stalk. Then cut back the stalk to the next leaf axil to promote more flowering stalks. For plants such as lavender, where flowers grow along the stalk, cut the stalk back to the main stem, as it will not rebloom.

Gently shake or stir the harvested flowers to encourage any insects inside them to fly away!

Harvesting in the fall is a matter of getting in a harvest before frosts kill the leaves. Perennial herbs can be snipped back to the crown (except for lavender). Annual plants can be removed entirely and hung upside down to dry—roots, leaves, and all.[1]—JM

Fragrant chamomile flowers are a breeze to harvest and dry for use.

When is the best time of day to harvest herbs?

Generally speaking, if you're harvesting from your outdoor garden, the best time to do so is in the early morning, when the temperatures are still cool. This will help prevent the trimmings from wilting in the heat before you get a chance to use them. And, perhaps even more importantly, herbs are at their most flavourful in the morning, as the heat of the day will evaporate their tasty, volatile oils. If your herbs are indoors, you have the luxury of picking and choosing when you want to harvest.—SN

How do I store fresh herbs? How long do they last?

Should you store your herbs in the refrigerator or on the counter? The general answer is to keep them chilled. There are a couple of good ways to store them for optimal freshness over time. Herbs such as parsley, cilantro, dill, mint, chervil, and tarragon can be stored in a clean canning jar or a glass filled with two inches (five centimetres) of water. Keep all the upper leaves intact but remove a few lower leaves so that they won't be sitting in the water (much like you do when you put cut flowers in a vase). Plop the herbs in the jar and cover the top of the jar with a plastic bag. Put the jar in the fridge and harvest the leaves as needed. Change the water every couple of days. The stems should last about three weeks.

Another option is to wash and pat dry your harvested herbs. Keep the leaves and stems intact. Wrap them in a single layer in a slightly damp (not wet!) paper towel and roll the towel up so that the sprigs are completely encased. Put the roll into a plastic storage bag and put them in the refrigerator in your crisper drawer. This works best with herbs such as thyme, sage, savory (winter and summer), and chives. They'll stay fresh for approximately two weeks, so be sure to use them up.

There is a major exception to everything I have mentioned so far: basil really hates hanging out in the fridge and should be kept outside of it. When you've harvested your basil plants, trim off the bottom leaves of the stems and use them right away. Prop the stems into a clean canning jar or glass with about two inches (five centimetres) of water in it. Store the herbs out of direct sunlight (but not in darkness), at room temperature. Change the water every two days. They should last approximately two weeks. (You might be fortunate enough that the cuttings start to develop roots and then you can keep them even longer!)

When storing your herbs in the refrigerator, be aware of the temperature of the appliance. Depending on the efficiency of the fridge and how much is being stored in it, the very back of the fridge can sometimes reach below 32°F (0°C). While you can freeze herbs, there are some very specific methods to do so (see pages 74–75) and you don't want to inadvertently overchill them, which may cause them to blacken and render them unusable.[2] —SN

70

Sage is commonly used in meat and poultry dishes and as an ingredient in bread-based dressings and stuffings.

I want to dry some herbs to store them. How can I do this?

Drying herbs is one of the easiest ways to preserve our herbs for use over the winter months. Done properly, they will retain their colour, fragrance, taste, and constituent chemicals.

The time-honoured method is to hang bundles of herbs upside down to dry. Simply take stems of herbs and tie them tightly together with string, rubber bands, or twist ties, ensuring that the stems will not slide out as they dry. Keep bundles slim, with the diameter of the bundle where it is tied no larger than a pencil eraser. This ensures good airflow through the bundle, which will prevent mould or mildew forming. Hang them in a well-ventilated but warm location out of direct sun. An airy shed is great, as is a bedroom closet with the doors open. Do avoid the kitchen as it is too hot and humid with all the cooking going on. Basements can be good if they are warm and not damp.

Another method is to strip the leaves off the stems and lay them down on a plastic mesh screen so that there is great airflow circulating above and below. Avoid using aluminum or other metal screens as the metal can change the taste and fragrance of the leaves as they dry. I have even used paper towel in a pinch, as well as baskets with a decent weave to them, making sure to stir or toss the leaves every day.

If you do not have a spot with good airflow, then using a small fan placed far enough away so that the leaves don't get blown away works very well. Or if your basement is too cool, then a small heater placed far away, just to add a bit of warmth, is a good option.

Dehydrators are often cited as an option for drying herbs, but if you do use one, make sure to use the lowest setting and check the herbs often to avoid overdrying them. I find dehydrating the delicate leaves doesn't give the same results as air drying. They seem to lose some of their colour and aroma, perhaps because the heat is so close to the leaves. I avoid using the oven to dry herbs for the same reasons.

After a week or two, check to see if your leaves are nice and crispy. Test a couple of the leaves to see if they have any moisture left in them by tearing them. If they are brittle and make crinkly sounds, and you don't see or feel moisture in the leaves, then it is time to store them in clean airtight glass bottles or plastic containers. You can also use paper envelopes and tape them shut. The one thing you don't want to do is leave them hanging or on the screens for too long as they will simply accumulate dust and, if humidity levels go up, will decay faster.

Use your dried herbs within six months, before the next growing season when you will be harvesting a new batch of fresh herbs.[3] —JM

One of the most important things to remember when drying herbs is to give them plenty of air circulation. Racks are very useful.

How can I freeze herbs to preserve them?

Sometimes your herb harvests are far greater than you can possibly consume in their fresh state; since you don't waste them, you need to save them for the future. Freezing is one practical and easy way to preserve the exceptional flavour of many types of herbs. There are several different methods of freezing herbs that may work for you:

1. Open (flash) freezing

Use with: rosemary, thyme, oregano, dill, bay, savory (winter and summer), sage, chives

How-to tips: Wash and pat dry the herbs. Do not chop them or remove the leaves from the stems. Place the whole stems on a baking sheet and pop the sheet in the freezer for a couple of hours. Then pack the herbs as is into freezer-safe storage bags and put them back into the freezer. When it's time to use them, yank the leaves off. (With chives, you can chop them while they're still frozen and add them directly to what you are cooking. You can also chop them before freezing them. If you're freezing lemongrass, definitely chop it beforehand!)

2. Freeze with water

Use with: parsley, cilantro, borage, mint

How-to tips: Wash and pat dry the herbs. Then remove their leaves from the stems. You can chop the leaves if you wish. Place a few leaves into the cells of an ice cube tray, then top up the tray with water and freeze the contents. If your ice cube tray has a cover, you can simply push the herb "cube" out of the tray when needed, and you've got an instant addition to the meal you are preparing. Otherwise, you can pop the frozen herb cubes out of the trays, place them in a freezer storage bag, and keep them in the freezer until needed. Warning: don't try this with basil. You'll end up with mush. Herbs packed in water last in the freezer for about six months.

3. Freeze with oil

Use with: basil, oregano, thyme

How-to tips: Wash and pat dry the herbs. Combine 1 cup (250 millilitres) of fresh leaves with ¼ cup (60 millilitres) olive oil in the container of your blender. Pulse until the mixture is smooth. Use right away or freeze the herbs in a freezer-safe container. Alternatively, some gardeners put a few leaves into an ice cube tray and add olive oil to fill the cell. The tray is then frozen and the contents are transferred to a freezer-safe bag. Herbs frozen in oil generally last six to nine months. Be very careful with herbs packed in oil; they must be stored in the freezer or a refrigerator set to 39°F (4°C) or colder, or they can harbour the toxic bacteria that cause botulism.

One huge drawback of freezing herbs is that they don't usually look very pretty when you go to use them; the process generally renders them limp and damp. They are best used in cooked dishes.[4] —SN

Summer savory freezes beautifully using the open method. If you've never grown and eaten this delicious culinary herb, it should be on your must-try list!

How can I preserve my herbs for use later?

Eating herbs fresh or preserving them by drying or freezing them are mainstays for using our herbs. But there are many other ways we can preserve our herbs.

One of the easiest ways to do so is by making herb butter, also known as compound butter, and with the popularity of artisan butters these days, this technique is sure to please. Butters can be made with a single herb such as parsley or dill. Or you can customize mixtures such as thyme, rosemary, and dill or other super-elaborate blends. The trick with herb butter is to use it within a day or two so that the fresh herbs do not render the butter rancid. However, it is as easy as pie to make a nice log of it, chill it, then slice it into sections and freeze the portions individually. Herb butter can be kept in the freezer for up to six months. Mine is always used up well before spring arrives.

Another simple method is to preserve herbs in salt. The salt acts as a preservative, and the herbs flavour the salt. Generously mix in freshly harvested and chopped herbs into a coarser salt, such as sea salt. Place in jars with lids screwed on tight, and shake every so often to get an even distribution of herbs with the salt. It will soon be ready to use and will last right up till the next season. Typically, savoury herbs, such as rosemary, thyme, and savory, are used with salt. Keep the jars of herb salt in the refrigerator.

Sugars, on the other hand, beg for sweet herbs, with lavender being a favourite. But do not limit yourself. Mints and edible flower petals are all there for the trying. Sugars do not need to be kept in the fridge as the sugar is the preservative, but do use them up within three months or the flavour will diminish.

Herb-infused vinegars are a delight. Add washed and dried herbs to quality vinegar, such as white wine or apple cider vinegars. Leave the herbs in the vinegar for a few weeks so the flavours will fully infuse it. Then remove the herbs or strain the liquid into another bottle, replace the cap, and use as you wish. Rosemary vinegar is popular but consider using basil, thyme, and even dill. In fact, just about any culinary herb you grow will make a delicious vinegar. Herb vinegars can be made using cold vinegar, or to speed up the infusing time, you can heat vinegar first before adding herbs to it.

The process is roughly the same when making herb-infused oils. You can use olive oil for sure, but any other oils such as avocado, flaxseed, or grape-seed are marvellous, too. Oils can be cold or hot infusions and can be stored in glass containers, preferably in the refrigerator. They should be used within one week. I make small batches and use them for drizzling or for dips and salad dressings.

When using other ingredients to preserve your herbs, it is important to use the best quality ingredients. Ensure your herbs are freshly harvested, wash them well to remove debris, inspect them for blemished or diseased leaves, and dry them thoroughly before using. Proper food-handling practices should be observed, with care taken to not contaminate your ingredients. Then enjoy the fruits (herbs?) of your labours![5] —JM

Did you know that you can candy the stems of herbs such as lovage and angelica? There are several recipes available online.

The Things That Bug Our Herbs

5

We cover a wide range of common (and some not-so-common!) pests and pathogens in *The Prairie Gardener's Go-To for Pests and Diseases*. We don't want to repeat ourselves, so you won't find any tips on how to deal with deer or rabbits here—they tend to leave many herb plants alone, anyway, due to the powerful volatile oils in the plant tissues. However, there are a few problems that many herb plants are particularly susceptible to, and we're focusing on those in this book. From recommendations for effectively dealing with whiteflies, thrips, and mealybugs to combatting powdery mildew and damping off, we've got your back when it comes to keeping your herb plants as healthy as can be.

One of the keys to maintaining happy, stress-free plants (*all* plants—not just herbs) is to ensure that you are doing your best to fulfill their needs. That means you may have to do some research. Plant labels and seed catalogues usually contain most of the information you'll need to site your plants properly and determine factors such as appropriate spacing, watering and fertilizer requirements, and harvesting tips. When the unexpected does occur, however (Slugs! Aphids! Leaf spot!), we use the practice of Integrated Pest—or Plant—Management to deal with the issue. Because we interact with our herb plants and monitor the way they look and behave on a regular basis, we usually are on top of a troublesome situation as soon as it occurs. If we think that action is warranted, we can take it, using the least environmentally harmful method to deal with the problem. For example, those slugs can be yanked off by hand. It's disgusting for the picker but highly effective and doesn't involve any use of chemicals. Moreover, the purpose of growing our herbs is to use them. Using any 'cide—be it an herbicide, insecticide, or fungicide—will contaminate the leaves and flowers of our plants. On the whole, just ensuring that we have a healthy environment where everything is in balance will be enough to ensure the health of our herbs. One note though: we sometimes need to be more vigilant inside our homes, and we may be required to take more drastic measures given the conditions in which we are growing our indoor herbs. Read on! —sn & jm

What on earth are those tiny spider-like critters doing on my herb plant?

Ever noticed your indoor herbs covered in white webbing and looking distinctly worse for wear? Chances are your plant has been infested with spider mites—arachnids smaller than the head of a pin that love to suck the juices out of our plants, both inside our houses and outside in the garden.

Spider mites are part of the Tetranychidae family (subclass Acari), and there are roughly 1,200 species to plague us. They love hundreds of our plants, mostly those with broader and softer leaves. Most commonly, it is the two-spotted spider mite (*Tetranychus urticae*)[1] that is in our homes, not that you can identify them by their spots unless you have a microscope!

The warm temperatures, low humidity, and dusty conditions in our homes are ideal for them to set up shop. Likewise, if our springs and summers are warm and dry, they will proliferate in the garden.

One or two mites won't cause a problem, but the fact of the matter is that one female becomes a multitude in days, as under ideal conditions each female lays up to twenty eggs per day and lives up to forty days. Eggs hatch in three days and young mites can be laying their own eggs in five days. Definitely a "yikes!" moment.

The first signs of a problem are leaves looking yellowish, or even just pale, just as you do when you are ailing. Look closer and you will see white or yellow stippling of the leaves where they have been pierced and where chlorophyll has been withdrawn. Leaves will feel gritty or dusty when you rub them, as the debris from the mites accumulates on them. Another sure sign is webbing that may or may not bind up leaves. Should things be truly awful you might see masses of the adults or eggs on the undersides of the leaves.

To be honest, if matters have truly gotten out of hand, the best solution is to lose the plant—fast! Spider mites will not be content with your basil and will swiftly move over to any other herb and the rest of your plants, for that matter. If your eagle eyes spotted them in time, then the first step is to wash the leaves off with water. If the plant is in the garden, a hose will do the trick. If the plant is inside, then lift the pot into a sink and gently rub the leaves while the water is running. Afterward, move the plant into quarantine and, if possible, into a cooler location, pruning off the most affected leaves. Keep the soil moist, but not wet. Mist leaves regularly and monitor for new activity.

If the plant is valuable, such as my fifteen-year-old bay laurel, and if more mites are found, consider using insecticidal soap every two or three days to ensure that all stages of the mites are controlled. Then monitor, and if more appear, repeat again. Be sure to really wash the soap off the leaves before you harvest any of them. Monitor the rest of your indoor plants, too.

In the garden, insecticidal soap can also be used, but beware, the soap will kill both beneficial and predatory insects as well as spider mites. I prefer to go with the long game and encourage lots of biodiversity, and generally those insects will do the work of patrolling and keeping things in check and in balance.[2] —JM

I think there are aphids feasting on my herb plants. What should I do now?

Aphids are everywhere, and always with us! The trick is not to try to eradicate them, because you can't, but rather to keep them in check and in balance. After all, they are food for a bunch of beneficial insects. But we don't want them on our indoor herb plants, nor smothering our outdoor ones.

Also known as greenfly or blackfly, they are part of the superfamily Aphidoidea, and may also be red, grey, or woolly. They can be born pregnant as they are parthenogenetic, a reproductive strategy that involves female gametes being developed without fertilization.[3] The result is many generations per season, and in bad years they can do a lot of damage, mostly to soft and succulent stems and foliage.

Now that is a sight you don't want to see on your herb plants! Spotting and controlling aphids before they turn into a complete infestation is important. Practise the Integrated Pest Management tenet of monitoring your plants on a regular basis.

As always, the key is vigilance and being able to act before they get out of hand. I am always peering at the stems and undersides of the leaves of all my tender herbs for signs of them. If I spot any of the ¼-inch-long (6-millimetre) bugs, then out comes the hose if they are outdoors and whoosh, off they go. Indoors, I will put the pot in a bucket of water and, using a softly running tap, gently rub off the bugs, at the same time giving the soil a good drenching, before allowing it to drain. Beyond knocking back the aphids, the action also washes away their honeydew, which can attract moulds.

Should they be persistent, you may need to resort to using an insecticidal soap repeated every few days to catch all the generations of aphids. Be sure to thoroughly wash it off before harvesting any herbs receiving this treatment.

Even better is to place herb plants in their preferred sunlight conditions and avoid overfertilizing plants, which encourages them to grow weakly and become stressed. This inevitably seems to attract aphids to them. When bringing any plant inside, accept the premise that there will be aphid eggs in the soil and always repot the plant into a new growing medium. — JM

There are some insects that look like tiny white flies on the leaves of my herb plants. What can I do to prevent this issue?

Whiteflies are a common attacker of both indoor and outdoor plants. Over 1,500 species of whitefly are found in the world, but two in particular are happy hanging out in our prairie gardens: *Trialeurodes vaporariorum* and *Bemisia tabaci*.

You'll have to look closely to spot these tiny white insects (not true flies) on your plants, but they are brilliantly white in colour so you can't mistake them. They'll often fly up in swarms if you move the plants they are feeding on. These relatives of aphids and mealybugs can be extremely difficult to deal with. In addition to causing feeding damage, they are also vectors for various plant pathogens, which means that as they chow down on plant tissues, they are also merrily spreading viral infections.

Whiteflies have sucking mouthparts that help both the juvenile and the adult insects take up plant sap. The leaves and stems of affected plants will start to form lesions and turn yellow, and the leaves may drop. The plants may become stunted in growth. Fruit-bearing plants may bear deformed fruit due to the enzymes from the insect's body that are passed during feeding into the plants.

Whitefly female adults can lay 200 to 400 eggs at a time. The eggs hatch a mere five to ten days later and the nymphs emerge, slurping up plant juices as they successively moult several times. (As a bonus, the nymphs also produce sticky honeydew, just like aphids. This may cause black sooty mould to develop on your plants.) The adult insects spend the rest of their lives eating and reproducing.

Control of whiteflies requires patience and repetition. If the insects are in their nymphal stage, take a damp, soft cloth or a pair of gardening gloves that you hate and carefully wipe them off of affected plant parts. Sticky yellow traps may ensnare adults. Ladybugs and lacewings love a good whitefly buffet, so by encouraging these beneficial insects to visit your garden, you'll have a decent solution for your whitefly problem.[4] —SN

There is a huge caterpillar on my dill plants. Should I let it continue to munch away or take action against it?

This is a caterpillar I positively love to see on my dill or parsley plants, or, in fact, on many of the species of the carrot family (Apiaceae) native to our area or grown in our gardens. I will gladly swap any damage they do to my plants for the striking butterflies they become, not to mention they are a most handsome caterpillar.

The black swallowtail (*Papilio polyxenes*), also known as the eastern black swallowtail or parsnip swallowtail, is found across North America in open fields and meadows, and increasingly on the prairies.

The adult is a beautiful swallowtail with black wings, with blue scaling and rows of yellow spots that are the most pronounced on the male. It starts off as a minuscule, round yellow egg on its host that hatches within ten days. The larva develops into a fat, two-to-three-inch-long (five-to-eight-centimetre) pale green caterpillar, with a black band covered with yellow spots on each body segment. This stage lasts from three to four weeks, when they do some serious munching. The pupal stage, when they form a dark grey mottled brown chrysalis, lasts for ten to twenty days, though if they are hatched in late summer they can overwinter attached to their hosts. The final adult stage, when we enjoy them flitting around the garden, is only six to fourteen days.[5]

A word to the wise: these caterpillars come with a "don't-eat-me" flag, namely a stink gland or osmeterium. If they perceive danger, even you just wanting to stroke them, they will rear up and out come two bright orange or yellow horns that contain a chemical that truly stinks.[6] An effective deterrent to being eaten or petted.

Should there be lots of caterpillars on your prized herbs, there are a few options to limit the damage. Simply hand-pick them off (with gloves on) and either relocate them or destroy them. Spraying plants with insecticidal soap or a strain of BT (*Bacillus thuringiensis*)[7] that works on this species is effective, though both will kill other insects as well and should be a last resort. Thinking long term, plan your garden with flora and fauna biodiversity in mind, as many other insects and birds love to feast on these caterpillars, regardless of their defences.

Me? I just sow lots and lots of dill and some extra parsley and enjoy what comes.[8] —JM

This is one type of swallowtail caterpillar that will turn into an important butterfly. Photo courtesy of Curtis Reynolds.

Some of my herb plants are sick and dying. I am noticing clouds of tiny insects on them—what are these things and how can I control them?

Thrips, also known as thunderbugs or storm flies because they often have mass flights during stormy weather,[9] are of the order Thysanoptera, which is 6,000 species strong. Most thrips species that bug us belong to the genus *Thrips*, of which there are close to 300 species, all agricultural and horticultural pests of varying degrees.

Thrips are minuscule, fringe-winged, pale-coloured, cigar-shaped insects that can look a bit like worms with legs. They can reproduce asexually, and populations can readily explode if you are not monitoring your plants. They are so tiny, they are hard to spot until you see signs of damage on the leaves from their feeding on the juices of your plants. Leaves will look pale, streaked, or mottled and drab, then will literally keel over since they cannot obtain water or nutrients. Thrips especially love chives and other members of the onion family but will go after any broadleaf plant. If you suspect thrips as the cause of your plant's suffering, then check the undersides of the leaves to see if you can spot them or place a piece of paper under the plant's leaves and rustle the leaves to see what drops off. Or use blue sticky traps as thrips are more attracted to that colour than yellow.

Thrips generally overwinter in plant debris, emerge early in spring, and get to work feeding with many generations per season if conditions are favourable. They lay eggs in tiny crevices in plant tissue, hatch in five days, and grow to adulthood within a month. It is best to encourage a biodiversity of flora with a multitude of predator and beneficial insects such as lacewings, ladybugs, and pirate bugs in the garden. If you have issues, clean up green plant debris, weed thoroughly, and pull back grass from beds as it can be an alternate host. Dry mulch is most effective at deterring thrips from overwintering and from successive breeding throughout the growing season. Oddly enough, given their alternative names, a good rainstorm will knock populations back, as will thorough but occasional waterings.

Thrips can also be vectors for viruses such as the tomato spotted wilt virus.[10] If you suspect this, then prune off severely affected leaves and put them in the garbage, not the compost. Then wash off the rest of the plant leaves thoroughly. You can also spray dormant oil on both sides of the leaves on susceptible plants every few days until populations are under control. Alternatively, diatomaceous earth can be sprinkled on the leaves. Water will wash these off, so both need to be reapplied after a rainfall or applying water. Insecticidal soap may also be deployed. But if a susceptible plant has been severely infested, it might be best to uproot it and discard the whole thing to prevent the spread of thrips to other plants. —JM

Get to know what the damage from thrips looks like. They commonly plague many types of herbs and other plants in your garden.

I am seeing white fuzzy creatures on some of my herb plants. What should I do about them?

Mealybugs are tiny scale insects, but without the tough shell or scale that protects their cousins. Instead, as members of the family Pseudococcidae, they protect themselves from predators by exuding a soft waxy substance that looks like cotton.

Usually found in warmer and moister climates than occur on the prairies, they mostly hitch rides to our homes and gardens on plants grown in greenhouses. But once inside our nice, warm houses, they can have a ball before we detect the damage they can cause.

Like all scale insects, mealybugs penetrate leaves and soft stems to extract the juices from plants, which can cause yellowing and distorted growth. They excrete honeydew, which can set up black sooty mould, and can be vectors for viruses.

The best cure is to prevent them from coming in by segregating new plants grown in greenhouses for a couple of weeks and checking regularly for any signs of damage before putting new plants in with the rest.

Ensure your plants are healthy by not overwatering or overfertilizing them, which promotes soft and weak growth. If possible, keep overnight temperatures at 60°F (16°C), which is below the comfort level of these insects.

Should you spot them on a plant—and they do love rosemary and sage—there are some actions to take to get rid of them fast. The first line of defence is to wash all the aerial parts of the plant, taking particular care to get the water in all the crevices where mealybugs love to hunker down. If that doesn't do the trick, the next step is to prune out parts of the plant where they are found, but if such pruning would kill the plant, then dab a cotton swab moistened with 70 percent isopropyl alcohol on the insects you find. Be careful not to burn the leaves. If the infestation is persistent but not heavy, then the next level of control is insecticidal soap sprayed on every surface every few days until there are no more signs of the insects. But if all attempts to eradicate them fail, then that herb or other houseplant must go out the door and into the garbage.

In our gardens, mealybugs are less of a problem as there are many predators happy to take care of them for you and our overnight temperatures usually keep them in check.[11] —JM

Speed is of the essence when treating mealybugs. If you wait too long to tackle them, your plants are likely goners.

My dill plants are deformed. What could be causing this?

A disease caused by a micro-organism called a phytoplasma and carried by leaf-hopper insects, carrot-aster yellows can affect many types of plants, primarily vegetables and flowers in the families Apiaceae and Asteraceae. If you're very unlucky, you may spot it in your dill plants, or perhaps lovage or angelica. It can cause new foliage to turn yellow, although the veins will remain green. The leaves will fail to reach their full size. Older leaves will become red purple in colour. The flower buds may not open, or they will become deformed, often sporting weird filaments in the centre that some gardeners mistake for fasciation — the abnormal fusion and flattening of plant organs.

Leafhoppers can become infected with the phytoplasma that causes carrot-aster yellows by feeding on a plant that has the disease. The phytoplasma takes up residence inside the bodies of the leafhoppers and quickly spreads its cells into the salivary glands of the insects. Leafhoppers feed by sucking on plant juices with their piercing mouthparts. They bounce from leaf to leaf, stem to stem, and as they open new wounds in a plant, they spread the phytoplasma around. When the insects move from plant to plant, the circle of infection widens. Cool, rainy weather exacerbates the spread; during hot, dry summers, you are less likely to see carrot-aster yellows in your plants.

Unfortunately, there is nothing you can do when your plants become sick with carrot-aster yellows: removal and bagging for disposal is the only way to prevent more plants from becoming infected. Do not compost plants that have carrot-aster yellows.

To prevent carrot-aster yellows, stop the leafhoppers from feeding on your plants. Cover your herb plants with row cover fabric to prevent the laying of eggs and subsequent hatching and feeding of leafhoppers. As well, remove weeds that are growing adjacent to your herb plants. Some of them, such as dandelions, are easily infected with carrot-aster yellows and the insects may hop over to your herb plants.[12] — SN

A white powdery substance has appeared on my herb plants. Should I be concerned?

If your herb plants suddenly are covered in a white dust that sticks to your fingertips when you rub a leaf or stem, chances are you're looking at powdery mildew. There are several different fungi that cause powdery mildew, including *Erysiphe* spp. and *Sphaerotheca* spp. As the fungi grow on their host plants, they form specialized structures that tap into plant cells and feed on them. That's why you might notice that a plant infected with powdery mildew might also exhibit distorted or discoloured tissues. They might droop or stop growing.

Pathogens don't work in a vacuum—they need favourable conditions to proliferate. In the case of powdery mildew, high humidity and cool temperatures are ideal for spore production. Hot, dry summer days don't usually encourage powdery mildew growth.

If you find your plants under attack from powdery mildew, you can trim off the severely affected leaves. Clean up all fallen plant debris. Watch how you water so that the fungal spores aren't splashed onto other plants or plant parts. If your plants have very dense, bushy growth, prune them so that more air can circulate within and around them. Don't crowd plants in your garden beds or containers. As well, cut back on fertilizing—particularly if you are using a lot of nitrogen—as the lush new growth is particularly appetizing to the fungus.

Some herbs, such as basil, mint, lemon balm, and rosemary, are more susceptible to powdery mildew than others, so if you find yourself fighting the fungus year after year, it may be necessary to switch up the types of plants you are growing. Most of the fungi that cause powdery mildew are host specific, which means that they will single out one plant to grow on and leave others alone. (Bear in mind that if there are several different types of fungi present in the environment, it may appear that they are the same type attacking all your plants. You can't tell the difference without knowing which species of fungus you're seeing.)[13] —SN

The seedlings I am growing have suddenly keeled over and died. How did this happen?

Have you ever gotten up in the morning, dashed over to your seedling trays in anticipation of seeing how much your little plant babies have grown since you last looked in on them—only to find that they are sick? The stems and leaves appear water-filled, and when you touch them, the stems are thin and mushy. Some have keeled over and the stems are blackened where they meet the growing medium. This is called post-emergent damping off, and it usually occurs just after the plants have reached the cotyledon (seed leaf) stage and are close to sporting their first true leaves.

Damping off is a common fungal disease that can spread quickly and proves fatal for newly emerging seedlings. Pathogens such as the soil fungi *Rhizoctonia*, *Botrytis*, or *Fusarium* cause the disease. (There are some water moulds that can also cause damping off, but the soil-based fungi are more familiar to most home gardeners.) Both post-emergent and pre-emergent damping off can be problems, with the latter happening before the seeds have even germinated. Sometimes when your seedlings don't pop out of the growing medium, pre-emergent damping off may be the issue. (There are many other reasons for this occurrence, however, so don't automatically assume that this is what is going on.) Once plants have become more mature, damping off isn't usually a problem.

Here are a few preventive measures you can use to tackle damping off.

1. Maintain strict sanitary practices when you are working with seeds and seedlings. Disinfect your gardening tools and containers between plantings with full-strength rubbing alcohol. This will prevent the transfer of fungal spores.
2. Never reuse growing medium that has been contaminated with the pathogens that cause damping off. Don't compost the diseased soil either; dispose of it in the garbage instead.
3. Make sure your growing medium has good drainage. Do not use garden soil when planting in containers. Many gardeners favour a soilless mix for seed starting as it may discourage the development of soil-borne fungi.

4. Plants need regular, sufficient moisture for their seeds to germinate and grow, but extreme humidity and overwatering will only promote the spread of fungi. If you use propagation trays with plastic domes, remove the covers as soon as the seedlings emerge to prevent excessive moisture.

5. Seedlings need plenty of sunlight. Aim for twelve hours per day. If you're planting indoors, grow lights may be required.

6. Irrigate with lukewarm water. Don't splash water onto the foliage of plants, as that may cause the pathogens to spread. Water at the base of plants instead.

7. Do not overfertilize. Seedlings do not need fertilizer until after several sets of true leaves have emerged. The seeds themselves have all the stored energy required to get the plants going initially. Too much fertilizer can encourage damping off.

8. Make sure your plants have sufficient air circulation. Take the lids off propagation trays for a couple of hours each day and set up a small fan near your seed flats. Allow it to blow gently on the growing plants.

9. Do not sow seed too intensively. Thin cramped seedlings once the first few sets of true leaves have developed. Crowding can encourage damping off.

10. Seed that has been inoculated with a fungicide is an option if you do not mind using treated seed.[14] — SN

Herbs for All Reasons
and Seasons

6

There is an herb for every place in your garden, and for every purpose and occasion that you can imagine. You just have to match that right place with the right plant and the uses that you have for them. We have mentioned many of these herbs in previous chapters, and indicated their botanical names the first time we referenced them, but here we will reiterate the botanical names as it is so important that you get the right species or variety for the purpose that you intend for it. Common names can be so confusing! —JM & SN

Which herbs do well in shaded gardens?

You'll notice we didn't write a companion question about what herbs are sun lovers. That's because most of them are! To produce abundant harvests of leaves and other parts, herbs generally need quite a bit of sunlight. Herbs that can perform in part shade, however, are less common. Here are a few that you can try in those semi-darkened areas of your garden.

* Chervil (*Anthriscus cerefolium*): I find a lot of prairie gardeners overlook this annual relative of parsley, but that's likely because its seeds can be a bit tricky to source. I have grown it in a raised bed multiple times and love its beautiful, frilly leaves, which are good to throw in soups (chuck some into your next batch of bone broth!).
* Cilantro (*Coriandrum sativum*): You either love it or you think it tastes like soap. (I am in the first camp.) Cilantro is very versatile and performs well in part-shade locations as well as in full sun. This annual tends to produce abundant seed if you let it, so if you don't want cilantro reseeding itself for an eternity in your garden space, don't let it flower and form seed heads.
* French sorrel (*Rumex scutatus*): Oh how I love the sorrels! (Ask me sometime for the recipe for my sorrel sauce.) These perennials are not only pretty but also extremely tasty and can handle part shade.
* Lemon balm (*Melissa officinalis*): This mint relative is an annual on the prairies, but I have had it come back in my garden, so don't be astonished if it doesn't completely vacate the premises, come winter. I love the flavour of this herb, so I don't mind that it is a bit bold with regard to its need for space. Shade conditions tend to mitigate its growth, but the trade-off is that more sun equals more leaves for tisanes.
* Mint (*Mentha* spp.): It will do well anywhere. You might not want that.
* Oregano (*Origanum vulgare*): This fragrant and tasty perennial will overwinter in most parts of the prairies.

✳   Parsley (*Petroselinum* spp.): I usually grow this biennial as an annual, but it can survive our prairie winters (most of the time!). I grow both the flat-leaved (*P. crispum* var. *neapolitanum*) and curly-leaved (*P. crispum*) types in full sun, but they actually fare better and give me bigger harvests when I offer them a bit of shade. —SN

Many herbs can be grown as microgreens, which means that they are harvested while they are still very small. If you are thinking of growing herb microgreens, the price of seed is a huge factor. Sometimes it's too expensive to plant a large quantity of herbs as microgreens. These chervil microgreens are seriously tasty, but cost prohibitive.

What are some good drought-tolerant herb selections?

Drought-tolerant herbs are often those with adaptions to prevent loss of moisture through transpiration, such as small, needle-like, fuzzy, or hairy leaves. They may exhibit a bloom or waxy coating giving them a greyish-green colouring. In many instances, such species have tough taproots or are a sub-shrub with their stems hard rather than succulent. Interestingly, plants with these adaptions are called xerophytes, which means they are able to survive, once well established, on available water alone.

With these clues in mind, here is a selection of such herbs, bearing in mind that seedlings in their first year are not as drought tolerant as those that have survived our winters and return come spring, making them star performers in our dry gardens.

* Blue false indigo (*Baptisia australis*): A member of the pea family (Fabaceae). Its long taproots make false blue indigo supremely drought tolerant, not to mention a net contributor of nitrogen to the soil.
* Dandelion (*Taraxacum officinale*): 'Nuff said. We all know this one survives everything, with its particular adaption to go dormant during the dry months.
* Lavender (*Lavandula angustifolia*): With those soft, fuzzy, silvery-green leaves, lavender is just a delight to have in the garden.
* Lovage (*Levisticum officinale*): It has a long, long taproot and needs water only in the hottest of periods once well established.
* Purple coneflower (*Echinacea purpurea*): Not only drought tolerant, it has long-lasting flowers and the seed heads are great for birds in the winter.
* Russian sage (*Salvia yangii*): It loves the dry and lean soils. Mine is right against the house, facing south, and thrives, a bit too well actually as I have a job keeping it within its boundaries.

- ✳ Sage (*Salvia officinalis*): It is really a sub-shrub, like lavender, so it loves hot and dry weather. Definitely no soggy soil for this one.

- ✳ Thyme (*Thymus vulgaris*): It adores dry, almost sandy soils along with full sun and withstands the heat beautifully.

- ✳ Woolly mullein (*Verbascum thapsus*): Known for its fuzzy, grey-green leaves, woolly mullein was introduced to America from Europe. It has naturalized and thrived, being variously considered over time as a noxious weed, wildflower, and powerful herb.

- ✳ Wormwood (*Artemisia absinthium*): It is highly aromatic and especially drought tolerant, but place it where children or pets won't be nearby, as it contains absinthin, a toxic substance that makes this plant especially good as an insect repellent. It is the source of the liquor absinthe.

- ✳ Yarrow (*Achillea* spp.): Not only does it stand up to the heat and the drought, but it is deer and rabbit resistant.

- ✳ Yucca (*Yucca* spp.): With its thick, waxy leaves, yucca is great for the dry section of an herb bed.[1] —JM

Beautiful echinacea is adaptable to dry soils, and as a bonus, it serves a bunch of useful functions in the garden!

I have a damp area in my garden. Are there any herbs that will work there?

Often, we view moist soils as being those in the shade, but that is not always the case. These herbs all prefer soils on the wet to moist side and can handle a range of sunlight conditions.

* Blue cohosh (*Caulophyllum giganteum*), a native of Manitoba and the eastern provinces, is found is rich, moist woodland soils. A perennial hardy plant to Zone 3, it is perfect for those damp soils with dappled shade.
* Chervil (*Anthriscus cerefolium*) is related to cilantro and as such prefers cool, partially shaded locations in damp soil. An excellent spring to early summer herb.
* Comfrey (*Symphytum officinale*), with its roots reaching six feet (two metres) down into the soil profile, can really handle damp soils so long as it gets lots of sun.
* Lemongrass (*Cymbopogon citratus*) loves lots of water. If it is being grown in heavy clay soil, be sure to amend with compost as lemongrass prefers a rich and loamy soil.
* Marsh mallow (*Althaea officinalis*) absolutely loves marshy, wet soils and is not fussy about the amount of sunlight it gets. Harvest the roots and make your own marshmallows!
* Mint (*Mentha* spp.) of all sorts when grown in dry soils really struggles, with a bitter taste and thin leaves, especially English mint and water mint (*M. aquatica*). If grown in damp to moist soils, it will thrive regardless of the amount of sunlight it receives.
* Scarlet bee balm (*Monarda didyma*) grows best in soils with a high percentage of organic matter that are consistently moist. The best example I have seen is a beautiful and large stand next to a waterfall where the soil was consistently misted!
* Stinging nettle (*Urtica dioica*) is well known for its hairlike hooks that inject histamine into the skin that can really hurt. Grow it in full sun to partial shade in any soil so long as it is moisture retentive.

* Sweet woodruff (*Galium odoratum*) is a lovely ground cover, with tiny, sweet-smelling flowers in spring. It loves a woodland setting with rich, moisture-retentive soil and dappled shade.
* Vietnamese cilantro (*Persicaria odorata*) loves sun but very wet soils. It can be grown at the water's edge like watercress or in super-damp soils.
* Watercress (*Nasturtium officinale*) is a salad herb that grows best in the spring along the water's edge with running water or in a really damp and shady spot.
* Willow (*Salix* spp.), even though it is a woody plant, needs to be included on this list for its herbal properties. Think Aspirin! Choose a species that loves a wet environment, such as narrowleaf willow (*S. exigua*) or Bebb's willow (*S. bebbiana*), but make sure it is in full sun.[2] —JM

Before you plant comfrey, ensure that you consider its aggressively spreading root system and propensity to vigorously self-seed. To prevent seed production, plant the cultivar 'Bocking 14', which is sterile.

I am interested in growing herbs for cooking. What are some good ones to try?

Before I deliver the goods on which herbs are popular for culinary use, here's a note about using dried herbs versus fresh ones: Fresh herbs are usually added to a dish just before you finish cooking. This maximizes the flavour they impart. Dried herbs are generally more concentrated in flavour than fresh ones, and they can be added to a dish near the beginning of cooking as you'll want the moisture in the food and the heat to bring out the flavour of the herbs. If your recipe calls for one tablespoon of fresh herbs and you only have dried, use one teaspoon of dried herbs.

✴   Basil (*Ocimum* spp.): There are so many different varieties of basil and each one has its own flavour profile. Many international cuisines, from Italian to Asian, use basil. From pesto to pasta sauce and curries, basil is truly indispensable.

✴   Bay laurel (*Laurus nobilis*): It's rare that you'll use fresh bay leaves in cooking, but dried leaves should always be in your pantry for tucking into stews and soups. This durable, highly fragrant and flavourful herb is meant for dishes that cook long and slow.

✴   Chives (*Allium schoenoprasum*): Truly, this onion relative is one of the most versatile herbs you'll ever grow and eat. It has a mild onion flavour that doesn't overpower dishes. Add it to pretty much everything you cook—you won't be disappointed.

✴   Cilantro (*Coriandrum sativum*): Commonly used in the foods of several different cultures—Mexican, Middle Eastern, Thai, Chinese, and Vietnamese—cilantro's biting citrus flavour complements many dishes. Once you've tried it, you won't ever forget the taste.

✴   Dill (*Anethum graveolens*): Honestly, grow this pungent, delicious herb just for eating with baby potatoes freshly dug out of the ground and gently boiled. Or use it in a myriad of other ways, including with pickled garlic and cucumbers, or sprinkled on creamy gently cooked egg yolks in devilled eggs. Dill makes a mean herb butter, too!

* Mint (*Mentha* spp.): Like basil, there are dozens of varieties of mint—from pineapple to chocolate!—and it's one of those herbs that cooks and bartenders alike love to use.
* Oregano (*Origanum* spp.): The warm, woody fragrance of oregano is one of my favourite scents. I don't make tomato sauce without it. It's also popular in Greek and Mexican foods.
* Parsley (*Petroselinum* spp.): I honestly couldn't do without fresh parsley in the kitchen. I use it in nearly everything, from egg dishes to soups and wraps.
* Rosemary (*Salvia rosmarinus*): This woody herb has stiff needle-like leaves containing intense concentrations of aromatic oils. Rosemary is used in an abundance of meat, poultry, fish, and vegetable dishes.
* Sage (*Salvia officinalis*): I can't make dressing for my Thanksgiving dinner without culinary sage—the combined sweet and savoury flavours that this herb offers are irresistible.
* Thyme (*Thymus* spp.): The tiny leaves of this herb are a powerhouse in the taste department! Thyme is ideal in pork, fish, and poultry dishes. Cooked potatoes and carrots really benefit from a sprinkling of thyme as well.

I have barely touched upon all the wonderful culinary herbs that you can try. Don't be afraid to experiment![3] —**SN**

It can be a bit tricky to source the seeds of little leaf basil, but the plants are bushy and compact and the flavour of the leaves is bright and bold.

What types of native herb plants do we have on the prairies?

This list is merely scratching the surface, as we could write an entire book on this topic alone! Many of these plants were historically used by Indigenous peoples for medicine, food, and ceremonies, and the knowledge of their value is still kept, shared, and practised today.

* Bearberry (*Arctostaphylos uva-ursi*, also commonly known as kinnikinnick): This evergreen ground cover with bright red berries is found in sandy soils in mountainous regions and in the foothills.

* Bitterroot (*Lewisia rediviva*): Diminutive bitterroot has succulent leaves and showstopping flowers in early spring. It is a low-growing denizen of the dry, sunny edges of woodlands and forests as well as rocky outcroppings.

* Fireweed (*Epilobium* spp.): If you've ever driven through the Rocky Mountain parks or along ditches or sites disturbed by construction or wildfires, you've likely spotted the gorgeous spikes of pink-purple blooms of common fireweed (*E. angustifolium*) in late summer. As this plant easily spreads by both rhizomes and seed, you'll usually encounter massive swaths of it.

* Fleabane (*Erigeron compositus*) needs a better name, though it has been well used to repel those pesky insects. With those finely cut pink and white petals surrounding a cushion, it makes a fine addition to an herb garden.

* Horned dandelion (*Taraxacum ceratophorum*): This isn't your average "lawn" dandelion! You may not be aware that there is a native dandelion found in mountainous regions such as Waterton Lakes National Park and even in the Canadian Arctic. Although the bright yellow flowers look similar, *T. ceratophorum* is shorter in stature than *T. officinale* and does not have an invasive growth habit.

* Labrador tea (*Rhododendron* spp.): Labrador tea thrives in boggy, peat-heavy soils on the edges of coniferous forests. There are two main species that grow on the prairies: Labrador tea (*R. groenlandicum*) and a smaller species, northern Labrador tea (*R. tomentosum*).[4]

* Milkweed (*Asclepias* spp.): This plant not only attracts butterflies but has been used medicinally by Indigenous peoples for things like wart removals as well as infusions to help with swellings and rashes. Beware, it is potentially poisonous if used orally without expert knowledge.

* Silver sage (*Artemisia frigida*): Also known as prairie sagewort, silver sage is a lovely perennial, with a woody taproot with stems branching out creating mats or clumps. It has been used extensively by Indigenous peoples. It can become weedy in disturbed areas.

* Stinging nettle (*Urtica dioica*): With a wide distribution all over the prairies, and even into subalpine areas, stinging nettle has tiny stinging trichomes (hairs) all over its stems and leaves, as well as fuzzy white flowers.

* Sweetgrass (*Anthoxanthum nitens*): This beautifully fragrant grass spreads readily by rhizomes, and not usually from seed. In fact, seeds collected from sweetgrass are rarely viable: germination rates are between 5 and 10 percent.[5]

* Wild rose (*Rosa* spp.): There are several native rose species that thrive on the prairies, including *R. acicularis* (prickly wild rose, the provincial flower of Alberta), *R. arkansana* (prairie rose, with pale pink blooms), and *R. woodsii* (Woods' rose, with fewer thorns than prickly or prairie roses). These thorny, deciduous shrubs are highly appealing for wildlife and pollinator insects.

* Yarrow (*Achillea millefolium*): Yarrow is ridiculously adaptable to both dry and damp soils and can grow nearly everywhere from disturbed roadsides to fields and meadows. Yarrow has feathery, silver-green leaves and bee-friendly white flowers with a warm, spicy fragrance.[6] —SN & JM

Bearberry is a highly attractive, mat-forming ground cover. It is evergreen, and if you're fortunate to spend time in the mountains in the winter, you might spot its brilliant green leaves poking out from soft blankets of snow.

What types of herbs are grown for uses other than medicine or food?

It is easy to think of herbs only in the context of their culinary and medicinal uses. Yet herbs have been cultivated for many other reasons over the centuries, many that we just take for granted.

Right off the bat, numerous herbs have been cultivated for their use as dyes over the years. Blue false indigo (*Baptisia australis*) and dyer's woad (*Isatis tinctoria*) yield blue dyes, whereas betony (*Betonica officinalis*) produces chartreuse. Comfrey (*Symphytum* spp.) creates a lovely brown dye, but fennel (*Foeniculum vulgare*) makes a mustard-yellow colour. Agrimony (*Agrimonia eupatoria*) yields a bold yellow hue, and feverfew (*Tanacetum parthenium*) produces a greenish-yellow dye. Lady's bedstraw (*Galium verum*) is coral or deep brick red, but madder (*Rubia tinctorum*) is garnet red. These are just a few of the possibilities. Given the interest in natural dyes these days, using our herbs for this purpose is making a comeback.

Herbs also yield fibre, especially bast fibre, obtained from the pith or phloem of non-woody plants. The fibres are separated from the xylem and outer skin of the plant through a process called retting. Indigenous peoples used their herbs extensively for this purpose, specifically common dogbane (*Apocynum cannabinum*), also known as Indian hemp, among many other names. Stinging nettle (*Urtica dioica*) and various milkweed (*Asclepias* spp.) species also yield useful fibre. Flax (*Linum* spp.) is well known for its fibre and is the source of linen. Hemp (*Cannabis sativa*), specifically those cultivars with low concentrations of THC, has been cultivated for its fibre for 50,000 years.

There are a multitude of herbs that are the basis for cosmetics, hair care products, and perfumes. Think of calendula, lavender, chamomile, nettle, rosemary.

Although scientific research into efficacy is ongoing, many herbs are purported to be useful as insect repellents and attractants. Ants won't cross a threshold where mint is sprinkled. Hyssop repels cabbage moths and flea beetles that will target members of the brassica family. Lemon balm is good for keeping mosquitoes off you, as is a bay laurel plant if it is near where you are sitting. Should slugs be an issue, just plant chervil and every slug in the garden will gravitate to it, and you can deal with them as you see fit. Dill is a well-known aphid magnet.

Of course, herbs can have a dark side, as certain ones contain harmful toxins or chemicals that cause hallucinations and worse. If a "wort" is healing, then "bane" is to be feared. Dogbane (*Apocynum* spp.) is great for fibre but is also poisonous to, you guessed it, dogs. Likewise, fleabane (*Erigeron* spp.) has been used to kill fleas, and henbane (*Hyoscyamus niger*) not only does in hens, but is a danger to you, too. Rue (*Ruta graveolens*) is also called witchbane and was hung up around doors and windows to deter witches. It also deters cats if you have a nuisance feline hanging around the garden. Then there is wolfsbane (*Aconitum* spp.), which was literally used to poison wolves.

Herbs—so many uses and functions. Our human civilization wouldn't be what it is without them.[7] —JM

Fennel is a visual delight and a useful dyer's herb. Here it is underplanted with nasturtium, a beautiful edible herb.

Henbane is a prohibited noxious weed in many parts of Canada. It is very toxic and personal protective equipment should be worn when removing it.

Which herbs will repel pest insects?

Companion planting is a system where certain plants are deliberately grown together, with the intention that one plant will help out another by serving as an insectary plant (to help attract beneficial insects such as ladybugs that will prey on pest insects), trap crop (to attract pests away from more valuable plants), or nurse crop (to help boost seed germination rates or seedling growth of plants situated nearby), and many other reasons. While the scientific community debates the true efficacy of companion planting, it certainly cannot hurt to have a "the more, the merrier" attitude to planting certain herbs alongside other plants to help deter pests. I'm certainly not at all averse to growing more herbs, period!

Herbs that repel insect pests in the garden do so because they contain particularly high concentrations of volatile oils that are released into the air when the plants are subjected to heat or touch. As insects brush against plant tissues or the sun warms the plant, the oils that cause the delectable strong fragrances that gardeners love irritate pest insects and—hopefully—cause them to vacate the premises. Plant these herbs as buddies with other, more desirable plants in your garden or simply be reassured that specific pests won't go after these selections.

If you're having issues with mosquitoes, try lavender, lemon thyme, lemongrass, rosemary, marigolds, and scented geraniums (*Pelargonium* 'Citronellum'). Basil is another option: it contains the chemicals estragole, citronellal, limonene, and nerolidol, which are reputed to work against mosquitoes.

Bugged by flea beetles? Use basil. Catmint (*Nepeta* spp.) is another one to try, as it contains a chemical called nepetalactone, which is purported to be effective against flea beetles.

Aphids annoying you? Attempt a fix with members of the allium family, such as garlic and chives. As a bonus, carrot rust flies and slugs usually don't attack alliums, either.[8] —SN

Which herbs have beautiful flowers or are grown for their edible flowers as well as for their herbal properties?

Don't assume that every herb plant has flowers you can eat; stick to the tried-and-true selections when it comes to chowing down on this particular plant part. Don't eat any edible flowers if they have been sprayed with chemicals or are growing on a site that is polluted or adjacent to a busy roadside or other location where they can be contaminated. Teach children to be respectful of plants and eat only those that are known to be edible.

Just as when you harvest herbs for their leaves and other plant parts, the best time to pick edible flowers is in the morning, before the heat of the day. Wash the flowers well before eating them.

Finally, if you're not using edible flowers for decoration, you'll likely want to use just the petals, as the sexual organs are usually not very tasty. The following are just a few of the edible herb flowers you can try—if you're interested in eating others, research before you munch, and enjoy!

* Basil (*Ocimum* spp.): If you let your basil flower, you sacrifice the flavour of the leaves you are harvesting, but if blooms appear, eat them! They taste like the leaves and are extremely pretty and delicate.
* Black mustard (*Brassica nigra*): I don't usually encourage gardeners to allow mustard plants to flower because when the plants produce seed, they can spread like wildfire and your neighbours might be pretty choked about it. The flowers, however, are hot and spicy and delicious in salads, and if you harvest all of them, you'll stop seed formation.
* Borage (*Borago officinalis*): These gorgeous blue star-shaped blooms taste like cucumbers. Float them in summer drinks or freeze them in ice cubes for later.
* Chives (*Allium schoenoprasum*): This perennial member of the onion family has delicious blooms that you can throw whole into salads, infuse in vinegar, or chop into egg dishes. And, if you're lucky, it will bloom more than once a year!

* Dill (*Anethum graveolens*): If you make potato salad, mince a dill flower into the mix. Or tuck whole flower heads into pickling brine when you're preserving cucumbers or other vegetables.

* Lavender (*Lavandula* spp.): Buttery shortbread cookies. 'Nuff said.

* Wild bergamot (*Monarda fistulosa*): This isn't the citrus fruit that has the same common name but a native wildflower and an absolute bee magnet. The flowers have a pleasant citrus-mint flavour and are usually used in tisanes.[9] — SN

This dill flower isn't yet mature, but you could still pick it and eat it, if you wished.

I want to bring butterflies and bees to my garden! Which herbs will help me do this?

Bearing in mind that any herbs that are grown specifically for their leaves are mostly deadheaded so as to prolong leaf production, there are still a multitude of herbs that we can leave to flower. These herbs are positively a bee and butterfly's delight, not to mention the rest of our pollinators from ants to beetles and beyond.

Here is a smallish selection of some common and uncommon herbs that will bring in every bee and butterfly on the block. You will note that some of them are also considered herbaceous perennials due to their super ornamental appeal in addition to their herbal properties.

* Anise hyssop (*Agastache foeniculum*) with its purple spires of flowers in August is a magnet for all sorts of pollinators.
* Betony (*Stachys officinalis*), an old-fashioned herb, is a member of the mint family and features spires of scalloped-shaped flowers in purple and white.
* Borage (*Borago officinalis*) is also known as bee bush. I never met a borage plant in flower that didn't have a bee hanging off its beautiful sky-blue, star-shaped flowers.
* Chives (*Allium schoenoprasum*) have those lovely pink-mauve balls of flowers in early summer that everyone adores. Snip them for yourself too once the bees have had their fun.
* Cilantro (*Coriandrum sativum*) can be left to flower for when it inevitably bolts. Leave it to attract the insects and then you will get coriander, the dried seeds. A double win.
* Comfrey (*Symphytum officinale*) is such a large plant but has delicate pinkish-purple droplets of blooms that draw in bees and other insects like crazy.
* Common yarrow (*Achillea millefolium*), also known as soldier's woundwort, attracts butterflies that love its disc-shaped flower heads. It's so easy to alight and sup the nectar.
* Fennel (*Foeniculum vulgare*) attracts insects to its feathery, aromatic foliage like no other herb. It is also a larval host for

butterflies. Grow two, one for you to snip and the other for the butterflies.

* Foxglove (*Digitalis* spp.), with their tubular flowers, often have a bumblebee or two tumbling around in them.

* Garlic chives (*Allium tuberosum*) are the white flowering cousins to regular chives. They bloom later, at the tail end of summer.

* Golden marguerite (*Anthemis tinctoria*) or golden chamomile blooms non-stop from early summer through fall.

* Hyssop (*Hyssopus officinalis*) is a small, shrubby pollinator attractor, with a mild camphoraceous aroma, courtesy of its volatile oils. I have had mine for years and love the delicate pink flowers come mid-summer.

* Motherwort (*Leonurus cardiaca*) is part of the mint family and has the same upright habit of growth as many of the mints, but instead of pink flowers, it has purple ones. It hails from Eurasia but has naturalized across southern Canada.

* Scarlet bee balm (*Monarda didyma*) is so aptly named. Bees just flock to it, if I am not mixing my metaphors here!

* Sunflower (*Helianthus* spp.) is not often thought of as being an herb, but it is, and the bees love to sleep on its disc flowers come fall. Hoverflies love them, too.[10] —JM

When you're selecting sunflowers for pollinators, avoid the pollenless types that are used in the floral industry for cut flowers. These male-sterile flowers can produce some nectar but they don't have any pollen.

115

Which herbs do hummingbirds love?

Herbs with heaps of nectar are the ones you should be looking for when trying to attract hummingbirds to your garden. Many of these plants have tubular flowers. Hummingbirds don't really feed based on fragrance, so the additional delightful scent of these selections is a bonus that the gardener can enjoy. Colour may be an attractant for hummingbirds, however; try plants with red, orange, or yellow blooms.

* Anise hyssop (*Agastache foeniculum*): Also called hummingbird mint, anise hyssop has long-lasting clusters of dark purple-blue blooms.

* Catmint (*Nepeta* spp.): Yes, it can attract cats, but if you don't have feline visitors to your garden, catmint is safe to plant for hummingbirds. They love it! The pale lavender-coloured flowers have a sweet, minty fragrance.

* Goldenrod: There are several species of goldenrod native to the prairies, including Canada goldenrod (*Solidago canadensis*), prairie goldenrod (*S. missouriensis*), sticky goldenrod (*S. simplex*), stiff goldenrod (*S. rigida*), and northern goldenrod (*S. multiradiata*). If you want to add more native wildflowers to your garden, especially those that bloom late in the season, goldenrod is a good choice. Bear in mind that, like many other native wildflowers, goldenrod will reseed itself and spread. If you like the riotous splendour of meadow gardens, this is a good selection—and hummingbirds will give it a seal of approval!

* Lavender (*Lavandula* spp.): This favourite of gardeners ticks all the boxes for hummingbirds with its nectar-rich, tubular flowers.

* Pineapple sage (*Salvia elegans*): An annual on the prairies, pineapple sage might be a bit tricky to find in garden centres, but its bright red tubular flowers borne on slender stems and pineapple-scented leaves make it a standout for gardeners and an attractive destination for hummingbirds and other pollinators such as bees and butterflies. The blooms appear in late summer.

* Scarlet bee balm (*Monarda didyma*): I love the slightly messy pompom flower heads of bee balm. This species has bright red, two-lipped, tubular blooms.[11] —SN

Hummingbirds aren't the only creatures enamoured of anise hyssop.

Which herbs are commonly grown for herbal teas or tisanes?

Before we go any further, let's discuss terminology. I grew up on a good cup of black tea, strong enough that the tannin in the leaves permanently stained our teapot. Therefore, I place a real emphasis on tea being infusions made from the leaves of the tea plant (*Camellia sinensis*), be they black, green, or white, from oolong and good old pekoe to Ceylon. When we use the flowers, leaves, stems, bark, berries, seeds, or roots of any plant other than tea, then they should be referred to as tisanes. Additionally, tea contains caffeine whereas any of the tisanes do not unless they are included in a mixture with tea. Besides the botanical distinction, I don't even call them herbal teas because that just adds to the confusion!

Okay, rant done. Now, we can discuss the world of tisanes that can calm us or heal us, and that just plain taste great besides being fun to grow, harvest, and make into delicious concoctions. Here are just some of the herbs we can easily grow toward that goal, plus one (stevia) to sweeten that tisane if you wish.

Note: As we've mentioned earlier in this book, neither Sheryl nor I are herbalists, but we consume these tisanes for their reputed benefits. Consult with your medical practitioner, and please do your research before consuming quantities of any tisane for any reason, as many properties can counteract or interfere with medications you might be taking. Even if you are pill-free, know what the benefits and downsides of any herb will be. As we have said before: Herbs demand our respect!

* Basil (*Ocimum basilicum*) is good on its own or mixed together with lemon balm or lemon verbena.
* Calendula (*Calendula officinalis*) is used for its antioxidant and anti-inflammatory properties.
* Echinacea/purple coneflower (*Echinacea purpurea*) soothes a sore throat and aches and pains from a cold or flu.
* Garden thyme (*Thymus* spp.) is excellent for sore throats and generally fighting off bugs.
* German chamomile (*Matricaria recutita*) is well known for its calming attributes and helping one get a good night's sleep.

* Lavender (*Lavandula angustifolia*) has long been used to cure insomnia.
* Lemon balm (*Melissa officinalis*) is good for calming and reducing stress.
* Lemongrass (*Cymbopogon citratus*), besides tasting great, reduces cholesterol and improves blood sugar levels.
* Lemon verbena (*Aloysia citriodora*) is good for alleviating digestive troubles.
* Mint (*Mentha* spp.) is a digestive, not to mention just a lovely tisane to sip over ice on a hot afternoon.
* Red clover (*Trifolium pratense*) or crimson clover (*T. incarnatum*) are mild diuretics.
* Rosemary (*Salvia rosmarinus*) is reputed to support healthy gut bacteria, not to mention being great at reducing uncomfortable bloating.
* Scarlet bee balm (*Monarda didyma*) seems to help if you have a cold or the flu as it has antimicrobial properties.
* Stevia (*Stevia rebaudiana*) is our sweetener of choice. It contains compounds that are many times sweeter than sugar. Slip a leaf or two in your tisane and there is no need for sugar.
* Stinging nettle (*Urtica dioica*) is just great for those who suffer from arthritis. I drink it by the gallon.
* Tulsi (*Ocimum tenuiflorum*), also known as holy basil, has anti-inflammatory properties.[12] —JM

Lemon balm is a highly fragrant and attractive member of the mint family.

To make a tisane, gather fresh herbs and wash them off carefully. Place them loose in a teapot or saucepan or squish them up in a metal diffusion ball if you prefer. Pour boiling water over them and steep until the desired strength is reached. I like my tisanes without sweeteners or cream, but depending on your preferences either or both add to the flavour of any tisane.—JM

Tulsi has a warm, spicy flavour that is delicious either on its own or in a blended herb tisane.

Remember, when you harvest herbs such as this red clover for tisanes, ensure the plants you source have not been sprayed with any chemicals and that they are free of pollutants.

Which herbs are grown for their outstanding fragrances?

Want to induce instant happiness? Brush your hands against a fragrant herb while you're working in the garden and inhale the incredible scent of the volatile oils in the leaves, stems, and flowers. We all know about the benefits of aromatherapy, and many herbs deliver it in spades. Some of these delightfully scented herbs also impart delicious flavour to food, while others are useful in crafts, home decor, and body care products.

* Anise hyssop (*Agastache foeniculum*): This is a highly attractive mint family member with delectable, licorice-flavoured leaves and seeds. The seeds can be used in baking, while the leaves are excellent as a tisane.

* Basil (*Ocimum* spp.): There are many different types of basil, each with its own scent and flavour profile. Sweet basil (*O. basilicum*) is most commonly used in cooking, especially in tomato-based dishes. Holy basil (*O. tenuiflorum*) has a warm, slightly spicy fragrance and taste. Don't stop there—it is fun to experiment growing as many types of basil as you can find!

* Lavender (*Lavandula* spp.): The fragrance of this herb is highly sought after by many gardeners for good reason!

* Lemon balm (*Melissa officinalis*): This easy-to-grow member of the mint family has beautiful, lemon-scented leaves that are commonly used in tea and add flavour to fish and poultry dishes. A good selection for a container on the kitchen windowsill.

* Mint (*Mentha* spp.): There are many popular mint varieties, each with its own delectable scent and flavour (think pineapple, apple, etc.), but peppermint (*Mentha × piperita*) is one of the most widely grown due to its versatility in cooking and beverage making. Keep mint plants in containers to avoid them spreading all over your garden.

* Oregano (*Origanum* spp.): Some oregano varieties are perennial on the prairies and feature highly aromatic foliage and beautiful flowers. Oregano also grows well indoors in

containers. Strongly flavoured Greek oregano (*O. vulgare* subsp. *hirtum*) is a favourite in many international cuisines.

❋ Rosemary (*Salvia rosmarinus*): In sufficient light, you can grow this gorgeous evergreen, woody plant in containers indoors. If you are lucky, you will be rewarded with blooms.

❋ Thyme (*Thymus* spp.): Several thyme varieties may be grown as perennials on the prairies. Fragrance-wise, one of my favourites is lemon thyme (*T. pulegioides*). I grew it in a former garden, and it was a delight to work around; my hands brushing the leaves brought forth an enjoyable, intense lemon scent.[13] —SN

There are so many lovely varieties of thyme! Orange thyme is an absolute delight. Grow it in containers so you can pass by it and breathe in the citrus aroma.

We would be remiss if we failed to mention scented geraniums as candidates for delightfully fragrant herbs. As a bonus, they have gorgeous flowers that last most of the summer.

Which herbs are considered "easy care" and recommended for beginner herb gardeners?

Herbs that are not fussy about their growing conditions are the best ones for new herb gardeners. There are many herbs that can adapt readily to less-than-ideal sunlight and soil, and even will forgive the occasional lack of water without being damaged too much. These herbs are also fairly self-sufficient in terms of obtaining necessary nutrients. They also stay put, keeping themselves neat and tidy for you to harvest easily and enjoy.

Although this is by no means an exhaustive list, here are some stalwarts for the new gardener and fallback favourites for those more experienced.

* ✳ Calendula (*Calendula officinalis*) is an annual, but what an annual! Just throw some seeds on the ground and they will readily germinate, and soon you will have lovely plants with loads of beautiful yellow or orange flowers to harvest for their petals.
* ✳ Chives (*Allium schoenoprasum*) is a must in any garden. A super-hardy perennial, it forms nice clumps that show new growth in early spring for early harvesting. Chives almost take care of themselves and reward you all summer with long green leaves and lovely pinkish-mauve flowers in early summer.
* ✳ Common oregano (*Origanum* spp.) is another perennial that is good to leave in the garden to overwinter. Like thyme, it loves lots of sunlight but is happy with just about any growing medium. Don't overwater it as it does hate wet feet.
* ✳ Dill (*Anethum graveolens*) is an annual that will easily self-sow should you leave a flower head to go to seed. There is no need to sow any more come spring. In terms of growing conditions, dill is very forgiving, but do give it as much sun as you can.
* ✳ Echinacea/purple coneflower (*Echinacea purpurea*) is a hardy perennial that is adaptable to most conditions but prefers full sunlight. If planted as a seedling, it will flower in the first season, but it will take two years to flower if grown from seed.

* Garden thyme (*Thymus vulgaris*) insists on lots of light but, other than that, thrives on neglect. You can even let it sprawl and creep and it will look and smell wonderful.

* German chamomile (*Matricaria recutita*) is a self-sowing annual that is virtually pest-free. Just give it lots of sun and it will adapt to any well-prepared soil. You will enjoy the lovely white flowers and be able to pick them at your leisure for a great herbal tisane.

* Parsley (*Petroselinum crispum*) is a biennial that we treat as an annual. Seeds take a while to germinate and have a lower-than-average germination rate, so simply sow a few more than you need, place a cover overtop the soil, and check for signs of germination. Once seedlings emerge, lift the cover off and you are off and running to a big harvest. To ensure big plants, provide lots of sun and regular watering.

* Sage (*Salvia officinalis*), with its soft fuzzy leaves and pungent aroma, is a favourite herb of mine. It loves lean, almost dry soils and tolerates drought remarkably well. Harvest it lots and it will keep growing. Mulch it in the fall and it will overwinter beautifully.[14] —JM

Calendula attracts all sorts of pollinators! We typically think of hoverflies as predators of other insects, but they are also efficient pollinators.

Are there any herbs that are great for use as ground covers?

If you have a patch of soil—perhaps beneath a deciduous tree or on a terraced slope, or if you're replacing part of your lawn—consider planting some herbs for colour, fragrance, or their benefits to pollinators, to control erosion, or even to use in cooking. Bear in mind that when I mention "ground cover herbs," I mean that they cover the ground. These plants are meant to spread, and they will—with heart. If you absolutely need to keep them in check, you can put up barriers such as hammered-in edging or pull up volunteers that pop up where you don't want them.

If you plan to eat your ground cover herbs (the ones that are edible, that is), ensure that they are completely free of chemicals and pollutants. Be certain that your pets haven't been using that section of the garden when duty calls.

* Mint (*Mentha* spp.): We've mentioned this one many times already. If you've ever grown it, you know it fits the "ground covering" theme very nicely and rapidly.
* Sweet woodruff (*Galium odoratum*): This is a wonderful shade lover with pretty white blooms and attractive foliage.
* Thyme (*Thymus* spp.): There are several types of thyme that can work as ground covers, and they offer beautiful fragrances and good looks, as well as massive appeal to pollinators. Bear in mind, though, that in some parts of the country, *T. praecox* (commonly called creeping thyme although there are other species with the same moniker) is considered an invasive plant and should not be grown. Check your province's weed control act before you sow seeds. Woolly thyme (*T. pseudolanuginosus*) and *T. serpyllum* (another creeping thyme species) are usually better choices.
* Yarrow (*Achillea* spp.): The sturdy, absurdly hardy rhizomatous roots of yarrow mean that once this plant starts creeping, it will go on forever. If you're good with that, you'll be rewarded with its lovely fragrance and the bees will be absolutely thrilled.[15]
  —SN

Yarrow forms an irresistibly soft, aromatic ground cover.

I love plants with variegated leaves! Which herbs have stellar variegation?

When you're growing herbs primarily for their outstanding foliage, leaf texture and colour are extremely important. When plant parts have more than one colour, they are considered variegated. This can be a natural trait or something that breeders have created, but either way, variegated selections give us extra options for enhancing the beauty of our gardens.

* Cuban oregano (*Plectranthus amboinicus* 'Variegatus'): This isn't your standard oregano! This annual with white-and-green succulent leaves performs best in part shade and dry soils. Use it sparingly in meat and bean dishes so that its strong flavour doesn't overpower the dish.

* Ginger mint (*Mentha* × *gracilis*): Ginger-scented gold-and-green leaves and pretty pink blooms are standout features of this plant. Although ginger variegated mint is considered an annual in most prairie provinces, I still recommend planting any type of mint in containers, as they can be aggressive spreaders.

* Golden lemon thyme (*Thymus* × *citriodorus* 'Aureus'): The fragrant leaves of this dense, bushy perennial will lose variegation in intense heat, becoming mostly yellow. But it's still an attractive plant and is an extremely versatile culinary herb, commonly used in fish or poultry dishes.

* Golden sage (*Salvia officinalis* 'Aurea'): This perennial (to Zone 4a) is a compact plant that performs best in dry soils. It has beautiful green-and-gold, delicately fuzzy leaves. Golden sage is not as intensely flavoured as some other sages, but it can still be used in cooking.

* Nasturtium (*Tropaeolum majus*): All parts of this annual plant are edible, including the seeds. It has an interesting peppery flavour profile. The foliage of this particular variety has striking white, cream, and green variegation.

✷ Pineapple mint (*Mentha suaveolens*): So named for its pineapple scent, this mint variety has highly variegated yellow and bright green foliage. The leaves are round and soft to the touch. Warning: this is an aggressively spreading plant. We recommend planting in containers. —**SN**

Masses of tiny cute yellow-and-green leaves and a lemony fragrance make golden lemon thyme a standout in the garden.

Which herbs are massive and can serve as focal points?

We tend to think of herbs as being small, low-growing plants. Yet many are big, bold, and beautiful, not to mention productive. They can serve as focal points, create a fragrant hedge, and serve to provide privacy. So, whether you are designing an herb bed or looking to include your herbs in a mixed bed, keep these in mind and don't neglect the pergola either!

✳ Angelica (*Angelica archangelica*), a.k.a. wild celery or Norwegian celery, has been used over the ages in Nordic herbal remedies. It has a rather pleasant perfume, different from other herbs in the Apiaceae family, that attracts pollinators and humans alike. It can grow 8 feet (2.5 metres) tall with lacy leaves and the typical umbel flower. Its stems and roots are used in edible and medicinal preparations. Candied angelica has to be tasted to be believed!

✳ Banana (*Musa* spp.) is often referred to as an herb, mostly because it is an herbaceous perennial and not a tree at all, but what a large-sized herb it is! Related to ginger, the banana we eat is a fruit (berry), but the peels have traditionally been used to heal wounds and inflammation. They have other uses[16] besides providing comical accidents. You just never know when you will encounter an herb in the garden!

✳ Comfrey (*Symphytum officinale*) is also called the healing herb. Used to promote repair of cells in all sorts of wounds, it is also known of old as knitbone, boneset, and bruisewort. A big, tough perennial, it has thick stems and hairy, coarse leaves, and it forms an attractive, 4-foot (1.2-metre) mound covered in small blue, pink, or mauve bell-shaped flowers.[17]

✳ Common hops (*Humulus lupulus*) is a popular ingredient in beer, but it is also well known for its stress-releasing and insomnia-curing properties. It is also a fantastic climbing vine perennial that grows some 30 feet (10 metres) a year, and is perfect sited along a fence, trellis, or that pergola.

Meadowsweet has beautiful frothy inflorescences that attract pollinators.

❋ Horseradish (*Armoracia rusticana*) is a stellar plant for the herb garden with its large, banana-like leaves that are fully 3 to 4 feet (1 to 1.2 metres) high, with panicles of small, white-petalled flowers. While we use its roots as a condiment, it is also an herbal. By the way, the "horse" in horseradish refers not to the animal but rather to its strong or coarse taste and texture.[18] It is well named!

❋ Joe Pye weed (*Eupatorium* spp.), native to eastern North America, is a superb ornamental herbaceous perennial. Standing 4 to 5 feet (1.2 to 1.5 metres) tall, it grows into a dense, upright clump topped with dusky rose clusters of flowers. Long used as an herbal to reduce fevers, this plant owes its name to the Indigenous herbalist who introduced it to Europeans.

❋ Lovage (*Levisticum officinale*) is a pot herb on steroids as its distinctly strong celery-tasting leaves are a great substitute for celery in all recipes. With the plants easily topping 8 feet (2.5 metres) tall and 4 feet (1.2 metres) wide, I often think one is more than enough for a neighbourhood!

* Meadowsweet or queen of the meadow (*Filipendula ulmaria*) thrives in moist soil and alongside streams and ponds. With finely cut green foliage, crowned in August by delicate white flowers atop, it easily reaches some 4 feet (1.2 metres) or more and makes a lovely stand. The temptation is to put it at the back of the garden, which is a shame as the leaves and flowers are sweetly fragrant, though it is the root that is used as an astringent.

* Scarlet bee balm (*Monarda didyma*) is well known as an herbaceous perennial, with plants often 4 feet (1.2 metres) tall and almost as wide. We know it as a bee magnet, but it has been an Indigenous herb for aeons due to its antimicrobial properties.

* Tarragon (*Artemisia dracunculus* 'Sativa'), the king of herbs, is much used in French cuisine for its licorice flavour. Standing some 4 to 5 feet (1.2 to 1.5 metres) tall, it can make a fine hedge with its dense clusters of skinny green leaves and its upright habit of growth, if sited in full sun. —JM

This striking herb is not often grown on the prairies, but it should be! Angelica is beloved of insect pollinators as well as a delight to use in the kitchen.

What are some of the more unusual herbs I can grow in my prairie garden?

Gardeners adore having something unusual growing in their gardens, and never more so when it is a plant that serves multiple functions—tasting great and looking terrific.

Here is a small selection of some (fairly) unusual plants that we haven't mentioned anywhere else in this book. Plus, they are available as seeds or seedlings in Canada!

* Bloodroot (*Sanguinaria canadensis*) is a beautiful Indigenous herb, whose roots yield a deep red dye. It is also used medicinally for congestive issues. It's been in my garden for three years now and I love it!
* Dittany (*Origanum dictamnus*), also known as dittany of Crete, is a native plant to the mountainsides of that Greek island. It is used for dyes as well as medicinal benefits, and with its small, fuzzy grey-green leaves, it is a delightful annual for us to grow in our prairie gardens.
* Epazote (*Dysphania ambrosioides*) is traditionally used in Mexican and South American cuisines. It is an easy annual for us to grow and cook with.
* Good King Henry (*Chenopodium bonus-henricus*) is a pot herb, which makes sense as it is in the spinach family. Cultivated since at least 500 BCE, it fell out of favour by the sixteenth century but is making a comeback now.
* Greek myrtle (*Myrtus communis*) is more a houseplant than an outside herb. But what a plant it is, with its glossy green leaves and white flowers. In its native range, it is used for culinary and medicinal purposes.
* Horehound (*Marrubium vulgare*), a super mint, reminds me of sucking on a horehound candy as a child. This plant is a perennial down to Zone 4.

* Pepicha (*Porophyllum linaria*), also spelled pipicha, hails from Mexico and is a great favourite in Mexican cuisine with an intense flavour of lemon and anise. It is also called Bolivian coriander.

* Perilla (*Perilla* spp.), also known as shiso, is a highly aromatic herb from Southeast Asia. This is an easy annual to try growing.

* Winter savory (*Satureja montana*) has a lovely, peppery taste to it. Hardy to Zone 5, this is an herb that, if planted in a niche hot spot, will overwinter in Zone 4. Or bring it indoors for the winter.[19] —JM

The sight of the ethereal white blooms of bloodroot in early spring is breathtaking.

Fragrant, tasty, and possessing stunningly beautiful foliage, perilla is a great selection to try in your annual garden.

Acknowledgements

From Janet and Sheryl:

We would like to extend a massive thank you to the incredible publishing team at TouchWood Editions: Tori Elliott (publisher), Kate Kennedy (editorial coordinator), Curtis Samuel (publicist and social media coordinator), Paula Marchese (copy editor), Sara Loos and Sydney Barnes (typesetters), Meg Yamamoto (proofreader), and Pat Touchie (owner). A very special thank you to our series designer and artist Tree Abraham, who is the incredible illustrator of the book covers. We love being a part of the TouchWood family!

Thank you to Curtis Reynolds for allowing us to use one of his photographs.

From Janet:

Sheryl, as always you are the best co-author I can imagine! Who would have thought that this series would have happened from that one little innocent email all those years ago? While TouchWood Editions can only be the best of publishers for us!

Many thanks, too, to all the lovely gardeners who have picked up our books and found them useful for their own gardens. It is your questions that guide us throughout this series.

From Sheryl:

The support and encouragement from Janet, my family and friends, my library community, all our valued readers, the booksellers and retailers, and our colleagues and businesses in the horticultural industry have been absolutely massive. The gratitude I feel has left me without words (astonishing, I know!).

Notes

Introduction

1. Wiktionary (website), "Herb."

2. Oxford Learner's Dictionaries (website), "Herb."

3. Oxford Learner's Dictionaries (website), "Herb."

4. Comfort Keepers (website), "Herbal Gardening and Its Benefits"; Auguste Escoffier School of Culinary Arts (website), "5 Benefits of Growing Your Own Herbs"; McLaughlin, "15 Reasons Why You Should Plant Herbs This Year," Fine Gardening (website).

Chapter One

1. Cook's Info (website), "Potherbs."

2. Lima, *The Harrowsmith Illustrated Book of Herbs*, 32–35.

3. Sagouspe, "A Guide to Herb Spirals," Rise (website); Jabbour, "Build an Herb Spiral," Savvy Gardening (website).

Chapter Two

1. Renee's Garden (website), "Annual/Perennial/Biennial for Herbs and Flowers."

2. Dore, "Grow Your Plug Plants," Grow Veg (website); University of Massachusetts Amherst, Center for Agriculture, Food, and the Environment, "Transplanting Plugs and Grouping Plants."

3. Snyder, *Herb Gardening*, 171–77; How to Culinary Herb Garden (website), "How to Grow Herbs from Seed—a Guide to Success"; Mary's Heirloom Seeds (website), "A Growing List of Herb Seeds to Stratify"; Blankespoor, "Guidelines to Growing Medicinal Herbs from Seed," Chestnut School of Herbal Medicine (website).

4. Hartung, *Homegrown Herbs*, 122–23.

5. Snyder, *Herb Gardening*, 189–93; Lima, *The Harrowsmith Illustrated Book of Herbs*, 163–65; Gazeley, "How to Successfully Take Cuttings of Herbs," Grow Veg (website).

6. Lerner, "Propagate Herbs Now for Yearlong Enjoyment," Purdue University: Indiana Yard and Garden—Purdue Consumer Horticulture; Balcony Garden Web (website), "12 Herbs You Can Grow from Layering/Propagate Herbs from Layering."

7. Lima, *The Harrowsmith Illustrated Book of Herbs*, 162–63; Grant, "Dividing Perennial Herbs: Learn about Herb Plant Division," Gardening Know How (website).

Chapter Three

1. Garden Basics (website), "Watering Herbs: How Often to Water Your Herb Plants"; ECO Gardener (website), "A Guide to Watering Herbs—How to Water Your Herb Garden."

2. How to Culinary Herb Garden (website), "What Type of Fertilizer Is Best for Your Herb Plants?"

3. Hartung, *Homegrown Herbs*, 92–93; Levine, "To Pinch or Not to Pinch, That Is the Question," Napa Master Gardener Column.

4. Snyder, *Herb Gardening*, 218–19.

5. Stofko, "Which Herbs Bolt, Which Herbs Flower and Why It Makes a Difference," Buffalo-Niagara Gardening (website); Homegrown Herb Garden (website), "Why Do Herbs Bolt and How to Avoid Bolting."

6. Allen, "Should You Let Herbs Flower?," Sunny Botanist (website).

7. Toronto Master Gardeners (website), "Overwintering Rosemary"; Sweetser, "Overwintering Rosemary: Growing Rosemary Indoors," Almanac (website).

8. Okanagan Lavender & Herb Farm (website), "How to Winterize Your Lavender."

9. Iannotti, "How to Grow Lavender: Planting and Care," The Spruce (website).

10. Sakurai, "Perspective: Herbal Dangers," *Nature* (website).

11. Gever, "Hidden Dangers of Herbal Meds Reviewed," MedPage Today (website).

Chapter Four

1. Hartung, *Homegrown Herbs*, 116–20; Jabbour, "How to Harvest Herbs: How and When to Harvest Homegrown Herbs," Savvy Gardening (website).

2. Lopez-Alt, "The Best Way to Store Fresh Herbs," Serious Eats (website); Domrongchai, "Simple Ways to Make Your Herbs Last Longer," *Food & Wine* (website).

3. Hartung, *Homegrown Herbs*, 124–26; Kublick, *The Prairie Herb Garden*, 104–5.

4. Telkamp, "5 Ways to Freeze Fresh Herbs," HGTV (website); Government of

Canada, "Food Safety Tips for Vegetables and Herbs in Oil."

5. Hartung, *Homegrown Herbs*, 154–56; Walliser, "Preserving Herbs: Drying, Freezing, and More," Savvy Gardening (website); Campbell, "6 Ways to Preserve Your Herbs," Modern Farmer (website).

Chapter Five

1. University of Minnesota Extension, "Managing Spider Mites on Houseplants."

2. Loughrey, "How to Identify and Control Spider Mites on Plants," Garden Design (website); Oregon State University Extension Service, "How to Recognize and Manage Spider Mites in the Home Garden."

3. Britannica (website), "Parthenogenesis."

4. Iowa State University Extension and Outreach, Horticulture and Home Pest News, "Whiteflies."

5. Butterflies at Home (website), "Black Swallowtail."

6. Feinstein, "Don't Touch the Parsley Worms!," Urban Wildlife Guide (website).

7. Rhoades, "Bt Pest Control: Info for Controlling Pests with Bacillus Thuringiensis," Garden Know How (website).

8. Wise, "The Black Swallowtail Butterfly, an Ornamental Insect of Dill," *The Prairie Garden: Herbs and Spices*, 27–29.

9. Thrips i-D (website), "The Truth behind Thunder Flies."

10. Planet Natural Research Center (website), "Complete Guide on How to Get Rid of Thrips Effectively."

11. Hassani, "How to Get Rid of Mealybugs: 7 Easy Methods," The Spruce (website); Flint, "Mealybugs," University of California Agriculture and Natural Resources, Statewide Integrated Pest Management Program.

12. Utah State University, "Carrot-Aster Yellows."

13. Davis et al., "Powdery Mildew on Vegetables," University of California Agriculture and Natural Resources, Statewide Integrated Pest Management Program; Lutz, "Powdery Mildew on Edibles: Identification and Control," Greenhouse Grower (website).

14. Grabowski, "How to Prevent Seedling Damping Off," University of Minnesota Extension.

Chapter Six

1. Jeanroy, "10 Best Herbs for a Drought Garden," The Spruce (website).

2. Small and Deutsch, *Culinary Herbs for Short-Season Gardeners*, 57, 60, 69, 118, 159; Hartung, *Homegrown Herbs*, 204; Long, "These Herbs Are All Wet," Mother Earth Living (website); West Coast Seeds (website), "How to Grow Chervil"; Ontario Wildflowers (website), "Blue Cohosh."

3. MasterClass (website), "Cooking 101: The 15 Most Common Culinary Herbs and How to Cook with Them."

4. Food First NL (website), "Labrador Tea: An Abundant Local Edible Wild Plant."

5. Richters (website), "Sweetgrass."

6. Alberta Métis Youth Department (website), "Traditional Plants."

7. Wenner, "Native Plants for Textiles: 3 Bast Fibers to Know beyond Hemp and Flax," FiberShed (website); White, "Herbs for a Dyer's Garden," Advice from the Herb Lady (website); LiVorio, "12 Uses for Herbs Besides Cooking," Garden Savvy (website); Wilson's Garden Center (website), "Herbs That Repel Bugs."

8. Kanuckel, "10 Insect-Repelling Plants That Are Known to Keep the Bugs Away," Farmer's Almanac (website); Oder, "12 Plants That Repel Unwanted Insects (Including Mosquitoes)," Treehugger (website).

9. Albert, "Herbs with Edible Flowers," Harvest to Table (website).

10. Grant, "Flowering Herbs for Bees: Planting Herbs That Attract Bees," Gardening Know How (website); Snyder, *Herb Gardening*, 81–82.

11. Wild About Flowers (website), "Plants and Seeds: Browse by Latin Name."

12. Goodwin, "What Is Tisane? A Guide to Buying, Storing, and Brewing Tisane," The Spruce (website); Besemer, "18 Plants to Grow in Your Herbal Tea Garden—Blend Your Own Teas for Pleasure and Profit," Rural Sprout (website).

13. Chicago Botanic Garden (website), "Aromatic Herbs."

14. Carpenter, "Easiest Medicinal Herbs to Grow," Mother Earth Living (website); Jeanroy, "These 10 Easy Herbs to Grow Are Perfect for Beginners," The Spruce (website).

15. How to Culinary Herb Garden (website), "Which Herbs Make the Best Ground Cover and How to Grow Them."

16. Wise, "Giant Herbs: Ornamental Bee Magnets," *The Prairie Garden: Herbs and Spices*, 30–33.

17. Lima, *The Harrowsmith Illustrated Book of Herbs*, 136.

18. Stein, "Food for Thought: Why They Call It 'Horse' Radish," KNKX Public Radio (website).

19. Richters (website), "2023 Herb and Vegetable Catalogue."

Sources

Albert, Stephen. "Herbs with Edible Flowers." Harvest to Table (website). Accessed April 1, 2023. harvesttotable.com/herbs-edible-flowers/.

Alberta Métis Youth Department (website). "Traditional Plants." Accessed April 1, 2023. albertametis.com/app/uploads/2021/09/Youth-Department-Traditional-Plant-Flashcards.pdf.

Allen, Marvin. "Should You Let Herbs Flower?" Sunny Botanist (website). December 10, 2020. sunnybotanist.com/letting-herbs-flower/.

Auguste Escoffier School of Culinary Arts (website). "5 Benefits of Growing Your Own Herbs." Accessed April 1, 2023. escoffier.edu/blog/culinary-arts/5-benefits-of-growing-your-own-herbs/.

Balcony Garden Web (website). "12 Herbs You Can Grow from Layering/Propagate Herbs from Layering." Accessed April 1, 2023. balconygardenweb.com/herbs-you-can-grow-from-layering-propagate/.

Besemer, Tracey. "18 Plants to Grow in Your Herbal Tea Garden—Blend Your Own Teas for Pleasure and Profit." Rural Sprout (website). Last updated March 18, 2022. ruralsprout.com/herbal-tea-garden/.

Blankespoor, Juliet. "Guidelines to Growing Medicinal Herbs from Seed." Chestnut School of Herbal Medicine (website). Last updated April 27, 2023. chestnutherbs.com/guideline-to-growing-medicinal-herbs-from-seeds/.

Britannica (website). "Parthenogenesis." Last updated May 6, 2023. britannica.com/science/parthenogenesis.

Butterflies at Home (website). "Black Swallowtail." Accessed April 1, 2023. butterfliesathome.com/black-swallowtail-butterfly.htm#:~:text=The%20Eastern%20Black%20Swallowtail%20(Papilio,%2C%20Colorado%2C%20and%20North%20Dakota.

Campbell, Lindsay. "6 Ways to Preserve Your Herbs." Modern Farmer (website). October 16, 2021. modernfarmer.com/2021/10/how-to-preserve-herbs/.

Carpenter, Jeff. "Easiest Medicinal Herbs to Grow." Mother Earth Living (website). April 14, 2016. motherearthliving.com/gardening/herb-gardening/medicinal-herbs-to-grow-zmgz16mjzolc/.

Chicago Botanic Garden (website). "Aromatic Herbs." Accessed May 16, 2023. chicagobotanic.org/nature_and_wellness/aromatic_herbs.

Comfort Keepers (website). "Herbal Gardening and Its Benefits." Accessed April 1, 2023. comfortkeepers.com/articles/info-center/senior-independent-living/herbal-gardening-and-its-benefits.

Cook's Info (website). "Potherbs." Accessed May 16, 2023. cooksinfo.com/potherbs.

Davis, R.M., W.D. Gubler, and S.T. Koike. "Powdery Mildew on Vegetables." University of California Agriculture and Natural Resources, Statewide Integrated Pest Management Program. November 2008. ipm.ucanr.edu/PMG/PESTNOTES/pn7406.html.

Domrongchai, Alexandra. "Simple Ways to Make Your Herbs Last Longer." *Food & Wine* (website). Last updated January 9, 2023. foodandwine.com /seasonings/herbs/how-to-store-fresh-herbs.

Dore, Jeremy. "Grow Your Own Plug Plants." Grow Veg (website). March 27, 2009. growveg.com/guides/grow-your-own-plug-plants/.

ECO Gardener (website). "A Guide to Watering Herbs—How to Water Your Herb Garden." September 22, 2021. ecogardener.com/blogs/news/watering-herbs-best -practices#:~:text=Check%20the%20soil%20for%20moisture,season%20or%20 seasons%20of%20drought.

Feinstein, Julie. "Don't Touch the Parsley Worms!" Urban Wildlife Guide (website). September 4, 2010. urbanwildlifeguide.net/2010/09/dont-touch-parsley -worms.html.

Flint, M.L. "Mealybugs." University of California Agriculture and Natural Resources, Statewide Integrated Pest Management Program. March 2016. ipm.ucanr.edu/PMG/PESTNOTES/pn74174.html.

Food First NL (website). "Labrador Tea: An Abundant Local Edible Wild Plant." Accessed April 1, 2023. foodfirstnl.ca/rcr-archive/2013/07/labrador-tea-an-abundant -local-edible-wild-plant.

Garden Basics (website). "Watering Herbs: How Often to Water Your Herb Plants." December 18, 2021. garden-basics.com/watering-herb-plants/.

Gazeley, Helen. "How to Successfully Take Cuttings of Herbs." Grow Veg (website). March 16, 2012. growveg.com/guides/how-to-successfully-take-cuttings -of-herbs/.

Gever, John. "Hidden Dangers of Herbal Meds Reviewed." MedPage Today (website). February 1, 2010. medpagetoday.com/primarycare /alternativemedicine/18244.

Goodwin, Lindsey. "What Is Tisane? A Guide to Buying, Storing, and Brewing Tisane." The Spruce (website). Last updated February 8, 2023. thespruceeats.com /tisane-herbal-infusion-basics-766322.

Government of Canada. "Food Safety Tips for Vegetables and Herbs in Oil." Updated February 8, 2013. canada.ca/en/health-canada/services/food-safety -fruits-vegetables/food-safety-tips-vegetables-herbs-oil.html.

Grabowski, Michelle. "How to Prevent Seedling Damping Off." University of Minnesota Extension. Updated 2018. extension.umn.edu/solve-problem /how-prevent-seedling-damping.

Grant, Amy. "Dividing Perennial Herbs: Learn about Herb Plant Division." Gardening Know How (website). Last updated August 15, 2022. gardeningknowhow.com/edible/herbs/hgen/dividing-perennial-herbs.htm.

———. "Flowering Herbs for Bees: Planting Herbs That Attract Bees." Gardening Know How (website). November 29, 2022. gardeningknowhow.com/edible/herbs /hgen/flowering-herbs-for-bees.htm.

Hartung, Tammi. *Homegrown Herbs: A Complete Guide to Growing, Using, and Enjoying More Than 100 Herbs*. North Adams, MA: Storey Publishing, 2011.

Hassani, Nadia. "How to Get Rid of Mealybugs: 7 Easy Methods." The Spruce (website). Last updated May 8, 2023. thespruce.com/how-to-control -mealybugs-1902890.

Homegrown Herb Garden (website). "Why Do Herbs Bolt and How to Avoid Bolting." Accessed April 1, 2023. homegrownherbgarden.com/2020/06/why-do -herbs-bolt-how-to-avoid-bolting/.

How to Culinary Herb Garden (website). "How to Grow Herbs from Seed—a Guide to Success." Last updated February 15, 2022. howtoculinaryherbgarden .com/growing-herbs-from-seed/.

———. "What Type of Fertilizer Is Best for Your Herb Plants?" Last updated February 13, 2022. howtoculinaryherbgarden.com/fertilizer-for-herbs /#:~:text=What%20Types%20Of%20Fertilizer%20Are,excellent%20organic %20fertilizer%20for%20herbs.

———. "Which Herbs Make the Best Ground Cover and How to Grow Them." Last updated June 20, 2022. howtoculinaryherbgarden.com/ground-cover-herbs/.

Iannotti, Marie. "How to Grow Lavender: Planting and Care." The Spruce (website). Last updated July 29, 2022. thespruce.com/growing-lavender-1402779.

Iowa State University Extension and Outreach, Horticulture and Home Pest News. "Whiteflies." Accessed April 1, 2023. hortnews.extension.iastate.edu/whiteflies.

Jabbour, Niki. "Build an Herb Spiral." Savvy Gardening (website). Accessed April 1, 2023. savvygardening.com/herb-spiral/.

———. "How to Harvest Herbs: How and When to Harvest Homegrown Herbs." Savvy Gardening (website). Accessed April 1, 2023. savvygardening.com/how-to -harvest-herbs/.

Jeanroy, Amy. "10 Best Herbs for a Drought Garden." The Spruce (website). Last updated July 27, 2021. thespruce.com/herbs-for-a-drought-garden-1762032.

———. "These 10 Easy Herbs to Grow Are Perfect for Beginners." The Spruce (website). Last updated July 8, 2021. thespruce.com/grow-an-herb-garden-that-wont -die-1762037.

Kanuckel, Amber. "10 Insect-Repelling Plants That Are Known to Keep the Bugs Away." Farmer's Almanac (website). Last updated May 17, 2023. farmersalmanac .com/what-to-plant-to-keep-bugs-away-24734.

Kublick, Lyn. *The Prairie Herb Garden*. Regina: Western Producer Prairie Books, 1990.

Lerner, Rosie. "Propagate Herbs Now for Yearlong Enjoyment." Purdue University: Indiana Yard and Garden—Purdue Consumer Horticulture. Accessed April 1, 2023. purdue.edu/hla/sites/yardandgarden/propagate-herbs-now-for -yearlong-enjoyment/#:~:text=Some%20herbs%2C%20including%20mint%2C%20 lemon,to%20survive%20on%20its%20own.

Levine, Denise. "To Pinch or Not to Pinch, That Is the Question." Napa Master Gardener Column. April 20, 2018. ucanr.edu/blogs/blogcore/postdetail .cfm?postnum=26939.

Lima, Patrick. *The Harrowsmith Illustrated Book of Herbs*. Columbia, SC: Camden House Publishing, 1994.

LiVorio, Gina. "12 Uses for Herbs Besides Cooking." Garden Savvy (website). December 30, 2021. gardensavvy.com/gardening-blog/news/12-uses-for-herbs -besides-cooking/.

Long, Jim. "These Herbs Are All Wet." Mother Earth Living (website). December 1, 2004. motherearthliving.com/gardening/These-Herbs-are-All-Wet/.

Lopez-Alt, J. Kenji. "The Best Way to Store Fresh Herbs." Serious Eats (website). Updated October 25, 2019. https://www.seriouseats.com/the-best-way-to-store-fresh -herbs-parsley-cilantro-dill-basil#:~:text=Store%20hardy%20herbs%20by%20 arranging,Store%20in%20the%20refrigerator.

Loughrey, Janet. "How to Identify and Control Spider Mites on Plants." Garden Design (website). Accessed April 1, 2023. gardendesign.com/how-to/spider-mites .html.

Lutz, Joanne. "Powdery Mildew on Edibles: Identification and Control." Greenhouse Grower (website). March 27, 2014. greenhousegrower.com/crops /vegetables/powdery-mildew-on-edibles-identification-and -control/#:~:text=Vegetable%20and%20herb%20crops%20that,lemon%20 balm%2C%20mints%20and%20hypericum.

Mary's Heirloom Seeds (website). "A Growing List of Herb Seeds to Stratify." Accessed May 17, 2023. marysheirloomseeds.com/blogs/news/a-growing-list-of-herb -seeds-to-stratify.

MasterClass (website). "Cooking 101: The 15 Most Common Culinary Herbs and How to Cook with Them." Last updated September 2, 2022. masterclass.com /articles/cooking-101-the-15-most-common-culinary-herbs-and-how-to-cook-with -them.

McLaughlin, Chris. "15 Reasons Why You Should Plant Herbs This Year." Fine Gardening (website). Accessed April 1, 2023. finegardening.com/article/15-reasons -why-you-should-plant-herbs-this-year.

Oder, Tom. "12 Plants That Repel Unwanted Insects (Including Mosquitoes)." Treehugger (website). Last updated November 3, 2022. treehugger.com/plants-that -repel-unwanted-insects-4864336.

Okanagan Lavender & Herb Farm (website). "How to Winterize Your Lavender." September 13, 2018. okanaganlavender.com/blogs/news/how-to-winterize-your-lavender.

Ontario Wildflowers (website). "Blue Cohosh." Accessed April 1, 2023. ontariowildflowers.com/main/species.php?id=341.

Oregon State University Extension Service. "How to Recognize and Manage Spider Mites in the Home Garden." Accessed April 1, 2023. extension.oregonstate.edu /gardening/techniques/how-recognize-manage-spider-mites-home-garden.

Oxford Learner's Dictionaries (website). "Herb." Accessed April 1, 2023. oxfordlearnersdictionaries.com/definition/american_english/herb.

Planet Natural Research Center. "Complete Guide on How to Get Rid of Thrips Effectively." Accessed April 1, 2023. planetnatural.com/pest-problem-solver /houseplant-pests/thrips-control/.

Renee's Garden (website). "Annual/Perennial/Biennial for Herbs and Flowers." Accessed April 1, 2023. reneesgarden.com/blogs/gardening-resources /flowers-and-herbs-which-are-annuals-perennials-biennials.

Rhoades, Jackie. "Bt Pest Control: Info for Controlling Pests with Bacillus Thuringiensis." Gardening Know How (website). Last updated June 25, 2021. gardeningknowhow.com/plant-problems/pests/pesticides/using-bacillus -thuringiensis.htm.

Richters (website). "2023 Herb and Vegetable Catalogue." Accessed May 17, 2023. https://www.richters.com/Web_store/web_store.cgi.

————. "Sweetgrass." Accessed April 1, 2023. richters.com/Web_store/web_store .cgi?product=X6160&show=&prodclass=Herb_and_Vegetable_Plants.

Sagouspe, Tanner. "A Guide to Herb Spirals." Rise (website). September 18, 2019. buildwithrise.com/stories/herb-spirals.

Sakurai, Masatomo. "Perspective: Herbal Dangers." *Nature* (website). December 21, 2011. nature.com/articles/480S97a.

Small, Ernest, and Grace Deutsch. *Culinary Herbs for Short-Season Gardeners.* Ottawa: National Research Council of Canada/Ismant Peony Press, 2001.

Snyder, Melissa. *Herb Gardening: How to Prepare the Soil, Choose Your Plants, and Care for, Harvest, and Use Your Herbs.* Woodstock, VT: Countryman Press, 2016.

Stein, Dick. "Food for Thought: Why They Call It 'Horse' Radish." KNKX Public Radio/NPR (website). January 29, 2020. knkx.org/food/2020-01-29/food-for-thought -why-they-call-it-horse-radish.

Stofko, Connie Oswald. "Which Herbs Bolt, Which Herbs Flower and Why It Makes a Difference." Buffalo-Niagara Gardening (website). July 29, 2019. buffalo -niagaragardening.com/2019/07/29/which-herbs-bolt-which-herbs-flower-and -why-it-makes-a-difference/#:~:text=Bolting%20occurs%20when%20a%20 plant,not%20in%20a%20good%20way.

Sweetser, Robin. "Overwintering Rosemary: Growing Rosemary Indoors." Almanac (website). Last updated May 5, 2023. almanac.com/overwintering-rosemary -growing-rosemary-indoors.

Telkamp, Mick. "5 Ways to Freeze Fresh Herbs." HGTV (website). Accessed April 1, 2023. hgtv.com/outdoors/gardens/garden-to-table/4-ways-to-freeze-fresh-herbs.

Thrips i-D (website). "The Truth behind Thunder Flies." Accessed April 1, 2023. thrips-id.com/en/thrips/thunder-flies/.

Toronto Master Gardeners (website). "Overwintering Rosemary." Accessed April 1, 2023. torontomastergardeners.ca/askagardener/overwintering-rosemary/.

University of Massachusetts Amherst, Center for Agriculture, Food, and the Environment. "Transplanting Plugs and Grouping Plants." Last updated February 2016. ag.umass.edu/greenhouse-floriculture/fact-sheets/transplanting-plugs -grouping-plants.

University of Minnesota Extension. "Managing Spider Mites on Houseplants." Accessed April 1, 2023. extension.umn.edu/news/managing-spider-mites -houseplants.

Utah State University. "Carrot-Aster Yellows." Accessed April 1, 2023. extension .usu.edu/vegetableguide/root-crops/carrot-aster-yellows.

Walliser, Jessica. "Preserving Herbs: Drying, Freezing, and More." Savvy Gardening (website). Accessed April 1, 2023. savvygardening.com/preserving-herbs/.

Wenner, Nicholas. "Native Plants for Textiles: 3 Bast Fibers to Know beyond Hemp and Flax." FiberShed (website). February 11, 2020. fibershed.org/2020/02/11/native -plants-for-textiles-3-bast-fibers-to-know-beyond-hemp-and-flax/.

West Coast Seeds (website). "How to Grow Chervil." Accessed April 1, 2023. westcoastseeds.com/blogs/wcs-academy/grow-chervil.

White, Caren. "Herbs for a Dyer's Garden." Advice from the Herb Lady (website). Accessed April 1, 2023. advicefromtheherblady.com/herbs-in-the-garden/specialty -gardens/herbs-dyers-garden/.

Wiktionary (website). "Herb." Accessed April 1, 2023. en.wiktionary.org/wiki/herb.

Wild About Flowers (website). "Plants and Seeds: Browse by Latin Name." Accessed April 1, 2023. wildaboutflowers.ca/browse_latin_plant_name .php?firstLetter=s.

Wilson's Garden Center (website). "Herbs That Repel Bugs." Accessed April 1, 2023. gardencenterohio.com/herbs-2/herbs-repel-bugs/.

Wise, Ian. *The Prairie Garden: Herbs and Spices.* Winnipeg: Prairie Garden Committee, 2017.

Index

Page numbers in italics refer to photographs.

dock, 12
dormancy, 31, 35, 42
drought, 8
drought tolerant, herb selections, 101–02
drying, 72, 73
    air circulation, 72
    dehydrator, 72
    oven, 72
    storage, 73
dye, herb selections, 109

E
echinacea, 19
    drought tolerance, *102*
    harvesting, 68
    seed saving, 50

F
feather meal, 14
fennel, 9
    dye, *110*
    hardiness, 24
fertilizer, 46
    overwintering indoors, 58
    winter preparation, 56
fibre, herb selections, 109
fish meal, 14
flea beetle, 111
floating row cover, 31
    overwintering indoors, 60
    winter preparation, 56
flowers, edible, 112–13
    harvesting, 68–69
focal point herb selections, 130–32
forget-me-not
    fall sowing, 53
    toxicity, 64
foxglove, 53
fragrance, 64, 72
    fertilizer and volatile oils, 46
    herb selections, 121–22
    perilla, *135*
    watering, 44
    yarrow, *127*
freezing, 74–75
    oil, 75
    open (flash), 74
    water, 74

fungus
    black spot, 18

G
garden soil, 14
garlic, 9
    raised beds, 17, *17*
    scapes, 9
garlic chives. *See* chives
geranium, scented
    fragrance, *123*
    hardiness, 24
ginger, 68
greensand, 14
ground covers, 18
    herb selections, 126
growing medium, 14
grow lights, 30

H
hardening off, 57–58
    rosemary, 60
hardiness, 15, 24, 56
harvesting, 18–19, 68–69
    time of day, 69
heartsease, 31
heat, 8, 17
heat mat, 31
henbane, 110
herbs
    culinary use of, 7, 19, 105–06
    definition, 7
    design, 18
    economic value of, 8
    fragrance, 15
    larval hosts of insects, 18
    medicinal use of, 7, 19
    nutritional value, 7
    shopping for, 28
    spiritual use of, 7–8, 19
    unusual selections, 114–15
herb spiral, 20, *21*
holy basil. *See* tulsi
horseradish, 12
    replanting, 19
    reseeding, 53
    roots, fleshy, 39
hoverfly, *125*

© Steve Melrose

About the Authors

SHERYL NORMANDEAU was born and raised in the Peace Country region of northern Alberta and has made Calgary her home since 1994. A writer and master gardener, Sheryl holds a bachelor's degree in English, as well as a Prairie Horticulture Certificate and an Urban Sustainable Agriculture Certificate. Since 2013, she has served as the online Ask an Expert for the Calgary Horticultural Society. She works at the Calgary Public Library—besides gardening, books of all kinds are her grand passion! She is a small-space gardener (on a tiny balcony and in a plot in a nearby community garden) and she is most enthusiastic about growing veggies. She lives with her husband, Rob, and their rescue cat Smudge. Find Sheryl at Flowery Prose (floweryprose.com) and on Facebook (@FloweryProse), X (@Flowery_Prose), and Instagram (flowery_prose).

JANET MELROSE was born in Trinidad, West Indies, and immigrated to Canada in 1964. She has lived in Calgary since 1969. She is a master gardener and the creator and owner of the successful horticulture business Calgary's Cottage Gardener, which specializes in garden education and consultation, horticultural therapy, and advocating for sustainable local food systems. She holds bachelor's degrees in sociology and history, a Prairie Horticulture Certificate, and a Horticultural Therapy Certificate. Janet is a lifelong gardener, coming from a heritage of English gardening. She has a large garden at home in the suburbs of Calgary that can only be described as a typical cottage garden. She cares for many other gardens throughout Calgary through her work as a horticultural therapist, as well as a bed at the Inglewood Community Garden. She is married to Steve and has two children, Jennifer and David. Three cats, Patrick, Theo, and Mia, currently own their home and patrol against the deer, hares, squirrels, skunk, mice, insects, and assorted birds that believe the garden is theirs, too! Connect with Janet on Facebook (@Calgarys-Cottage-Gardener), X (@CalCottageGrdnr), and Instagram (CalgarysCottageGardener).

About the Series

You've discovered the Guides for the Prairie Gardener! This budding series puts the combined knowledge of two lifelong prairie gardeners at your grubby fingertips. Whether you've just cleared a few square feet for your first bed of veggies or are a seasoned green thumb stumped by that one cultivar you can't seem to master, we think you'll find Janet and Sheryl the ideal teachers. These slim but mighty volumes, handsomely designed, make great companions at the height of summer in the garden trenches and during cold winter days planning the next season. With regional expertise, elegance, and a sense of humour, Janet and Sheryl take your questions and turn them into prairie gardening inspiration. For more information, visit touchwoodeditions.com/guidesprairiegardener.